WHAT MY FAVOURITE TEACHER TAUGHT ME

A collection of
inspirational stories
selected by

ROBYN HENDERSON

2

First published in 2005 by Sea Change Publishing
©   Copyright Robyn Henderson

Robyn Henderson
What my favourite teacher taught me. Volume 2. A collection of inspirational stories selected by Robyn Henderson

1   Personal memoirs   2   Inspiration

2   Teachers and education

ISBN: 0-9752494-4-4

Printed by Watson Ferguson and Co
Cover Design by Unicorn Graphics

Sea Change Publishing
PO Box 1596,
Kingscliff NSW 2487 Australia
www.seachangepublishing.com.au
info@seachangepublishing.com.au

Contents

From Robyn

A Memo from your student

Stories by....

Author Contact Details

About Robyn Henderson and Sea Change Publishing

From Robyn......

The first book of inspirational teacher stories was a wonderful success and loved by all who read it. So many people asked me if there would be another book, or wanted to write their own teacher tribute, that this second volume simply demanded to be published.

There is something to be learnt here. Almost all of us have memories of the special people, places and events which changed our lives or gave us a glimpse of other possibilities to pursue. That word of praise, the positive re-enforcement that meant so much at the time, the firm belief by a significant other person that we would succeed—these things remain with us all our lives. Then there are those unexpected moments of clarity when we realise from something we have seen or heard that options are there for us—all we have to do is run with them.

This book could have been about the lessons we have learned, but I deliberately wanted to keep the focus on the people who taught us the lessons. Teachers are sometimes undervalued, taken for granted, and when we move on, they are often forgotten, except for those special people who entered our lives, made their mark and changed us forever. There are many stories like that in this book. Many of the authors whose stories you are about to read acknowledge that they are the people they are today because of the influence and impact of a particular teacher.

And of course, not all teachers are to be found in schools. In this volume you will read of teachers who are parents or neighbours; you will encounter powerful teachers in the form of adversity or even disease, and you will be reminded yet again, that learning never ends. To begin this book of stories Maggie Dent has generously allowed me to include a wonderful extract from her forthcoming book.

So, here it is. Volume Two.

More of the most inspiring teacher tribute stories you could ever hope to read.

To my Teacher—a Memo from your Student

Don't be afraid to be firm with me. By doing this you make me feel secure.

Don't let me form bad habits. I rely on you to warn me of their existence.

Don't nag as this takes power from me when I am learning to be responsible for my own actions.

Don't let my mistakes devalue me as a person. They are merely indications of how I can improve.

Don't make me feel smaller than I am. My defence will be to make you feel small too.

Don't correct me in front of my peers or other teachers unless you can do it with compassion and it is a lesson for us all to benefit from. I would prefer you to correct me in private.

Don't concentrate on my imperfections. It may lead you to overlook my strengths and talents.

Don't question my honesty too much. I am easily frightened into telling lies.

Don't be inconsistent as it confuses me and threatens my faith in you as a teacher.

Don't put me off when I ask questions or I will stop asking them. Sometimes I ask questions for those not brave enough to ask.

Don't suggest that you are perfect, infallible or better than me as a person. Knowledge of facts alone does not make a person superior. Please try to be honest and real as these qualities encourage me to be the same.

Don't tell me my fears are silly. They are very real to me and your reassurance and loving support will help me to conquer them and to grow and understand things better.

Don't treat boys and girls differently. We admire those who see us as unique and valuable regardless of gender.

Don't bribe me with rash promises as that threatens my trust in you and I feel hurt when I am let down by broken promises.

Don't assume you know how I am feeling or what is happening for me. That is arrogance even if well intentioned.

Don't pressure me to reveal anything I do not feel comfortable to share. Trust is a personal choice.

Don't judge me on account of knowing my parents or my siblings. I am a unique human being and I deserve the right to create my own relationship with you free of preconceptions.

Don't jump to conclusions on appearances when resolving conflict. Check both sides of the story before attempting to help us solve the problem. Watch my body language. It may tell you something I can't tell you.

Know that sometimes learning from experience can be messy, especially with paper, glue, clay, sand and paint—and the biggest lesson may be in the cleaning up!

If you recognise my pain or hurt show me you care, preferably in a small private way. I don't need a public viewing, it only adds to my anxiety.

When all else fails please keep a sense of hope that I am still a worthwhile person especially when I don't deserve it.

My final message to you is this—

You are very important in my life right now. You play a unique role in the formation of me as a whole person. Be careful when you share in my intellectual, physical, emotional and spiritual growth that you don't concentrate too much on any one area. I am grateful for your support and guidance in my developmental years.

Thank you.

Your Student

From *Nurturing Young Hearts and Souls – Building Emotional, Social, and Spiritual Competencies in our Young* by Maggie Dent

Shirley Dalton

Shirley Dalton *is the Franchise Manager for an Australian publicly listed education company. She is responsible for training, supporting and empowering franchisees around the world. Shirley is passionate about people and learning. She dreams of one day spending her time writing, travelling and speaking. Shirley's powerful story is an inspirational and challenging insight into how we can learn from pain and suffering, if we choose to.*

Her name was Clarissa and she was rotten, rotten to the core. There was absolutely nothing nice about Clarissa. She could be incredibly cruel and she caused a lot of pain. She made our lives a living hell. She affected everyone she came in contact with and yet, I have to say, she was my favourite teacher.

Clarissa taught me about love—unconditional, unending love. She taught me about compassion and she showed me that I was capable of things I never would have thought possible. She taught me that I can cope with anything, do anything. She gave me confidence and inspired an inner knowing so that, no matter what life throws at me, I can deal with it. I may not like it, but I can deal with it. Clarissa tested my resilience and my patience. Many times I wanted to scream at her, 'Go away, go away', but I knew she belonged to us and we had to make the most of it.

Growing up, Clarissa changed from being quiet and shy, almost unnoticeable to a torrid teenager fourteen years later. She would not be controlled; could not be controlled. Clarissa's temper was fiery at best. She would be unnervingly quiet, then, all of a sudden, she would flare up and let loose with her poison. We just never knew what she was going to do from day to day. We lived on tenterhooks.

Some days she would behave. Some days she seemed coherent, others, well, we'd rather forget. It seemed nobody could do anything with Clarissa. She had a mind of her own and her agenda was anybody's guess. We weren't alone in caring for Clarissa. We had the advice of many experts. We had the help and support of friends and the community. It was quite a humbling experience to have to learn to ask for and accept help. This was not something my independent family was used to.

As bad as she was, Clarissa helped all of us to come together, united in love. We learned nursing skills, counselling skills, cleaning and sanitising skills and above all, we learned to laugh.

Clarissa and I would often share a private joke. She would make up stories and I would encourage her by asking questions about the characters and scenes. I wheeled her all around the house as we looked for kittens, strange women and burglars. One night we even cooked fish for the tribes. Clarissa didn't know she was hallucinating, nor did most of the family, many of whom tried to argue and reason with her. Unfortunately for them they missed out on the fun. When Clarissa was happy, we would laugh and laugh. Her imagination was something else. So was her wit.

Each evening as she went to bed, we would carry out a little ritual. We would tell her to 'Say goodnight Dick' (from one of the old television shows). Clarissa would reply, 'Goodnight Dick' and wave as we wheeled her to her room. One night as we were going through the ritual she looked at my husband and instead of saying 'Goodnight Dick' she laughed and said, 'Goodnight dickhead'.

Clarissa is no longer with us; she died on 2 December 2004. Whilst I don't miss the work and the fatigue associated with looking after Clarissa, I do miss her constant companionship and the opportunity she gave me to go deep within myself to find the strength and love to be able to deal with her.

Clarissa had lived with my mother for fourteen years. Clarissa was my mother's breast cancer.

———————— ❧ ————————

Teachers are healers

Rod Matthews

Rod Matthews *is a highly sought after presenter, author and coach. He is the founder and director of Impact Publishing and Human Performance Technologies, a boutique learning and development consultancy. Rod lives in Sydney with his wife and two boys who make sure he keeps his feet on the ground and gets plenty of exercise. Rod has written a story which illustrates the importance of honesty, humility and self-awareness, and incidentally, provides us with insight as to why Rod is as successful as he is.*

I will never be able to thank the teacher who taught me this critical lesson. I don't know who he is. I don't know where he is. I was fortunate enough to be in the right place at the right time and to see him for long enough to learn the lesson I so badly needed.

I was engaged to be married for a number of years. The fact that I can't recall exactly how many years probably gives you some clue as to why the engagement ended. I was taking the relationship for granted. She got a glimpse of what she could be marrying and wisely decided to call the engagement off. I didn't see it coming and I was devastated. The picture you hold of your future disappears in the phrase, 'I think we should call it off'.

To make matters even more tragic, because we had been together for a number of years my friends had become our friends, and her friends had become our friends. This made it very difficult to visit the old haunts with the old crowd. She would be there. I wanted her back. She didn't want me. I would do something stupid to attract her attention. Everyone would become uncomfortable. I would leave. It soon became obvious that it would be best if I just didn't go to those old haunts or see the old crowd anymore. So I would sit at home alone on Thursday, Friday and Saturday nights while others in our group were making advances toward my ex-fiancée.

Are you feeling sorry for me yet? Please don't. I was just about to learn something that would not have been possible without this situation. For some very human reason you have to go to hell before you get to heaven.

After a number of months of sad, lonely, dinner-for-one, watching the least crappie thing on television type evenings, I started wondering how someone might go about finding new places, new friends and yes, perhaps even a new love. I had been out of the singles scene for a while so I wasn't exactly sure how to meet new people.

Then it dawned on me! I know what you do. You go to clubs and pubs, drink enough alcohol so it's socially acceptable to be a bloke and dance, and then you wait on the edge of the dance floor for the best looking girl to come up and ask you to dance. That's it.

And you thought the first bit was sad!!

And that is what I did. For the next eighteen months, I spent Thursday, Friday and Saturday nights visiting different clubs and pubs, drinking copious amounts of alcohol and sitting on the edge of the dance floor and waiting. Unfortunately, and to my surprise, no one approached me. So I would drink even more in the hope that it would make me more attractive. On occasions, I would actually get up and dance. A very unwise move as it is quite difficult to stay upright on less than twenty legs when you have had a bit to drink. Caterpillars, I'm sure, could get absolutely smashed and still dance, but it is beyond most bipeds.

If you have ever been to a club or pub you'll recognise this. The music has stopped, it's nearly closing time, people are leaving and there is this last guy who refuses to believe the evening is over. He has overindulged, he is unattractive, he is to be avoided. That was me!

One evening I was digging in yet again. I had made my home at the table nearest the dance floor in a club I had been ejected from on several previous occasions. I had a beer in one hand, a cigarette in the other and I was ogling the girls on the dance floor.

I looked across to the table next to me and saw another guy there who looked just like me, beer in one hand, cigarette in the other and ogling the girls on the dance floor. I thought to myself, 'If I was a girl, there is no way I would ever approach that guy. He could be a homicidal axe-wielding maniac for all I know.'

It was at that moment, the moment I saw him ... I saw myself.

I saw myself and it was not pretty. I knew that for things to change I was going to have to change. Since that day I have seen myself in so many other people. I have now come to call these moments a 'mirror moment.' Most of the time you look in the mirror with the intention of checking and improving what you see. Sometimes you look and you are satisfied. Sometimes you look and you are dissatisfied. This dissatisfaction usually leads to some sort of change.

And so it is with a mirror moment. You will see someone else doing what you do, saying what you might say, reacting as you might react. If you are satisfied ... great. Enjoy! If you are dissatisfied then keep in mind the following principles:

- It is possible to learn from others' mistakes. You've just got to notice when they are doing what you do, indeed, what we all do.
- Watch them with compassion ... it could be you!
- Use the mirror moment as the impetus to change.

Robyn Henderson

Robyn Henderson, *Global Networking Specialist, and incidentally, an associate, friend or mentor to every author in this book, has built a reputation internationally as a business educator and author, specialising in her passion—networking. As a highly successful self-publisher, Robyn recently took her business in a new direction when she founded Sea Change Publishing, providing comprehensive services to project manage books from their concept to completion. A master networker and acknowledged solution provider, Robyn is renowned for her innovative approach, her lateral thinking skills and her personal integrity. Reading Robyn's story, we catch a glimpse of where these character traits have come from.*

My father's business, the Australian Koala Bear Manufacturing Company, was located in the industrial suburb of Botany in Sydney. My father was one of only two people who actually made Australian souvenirs in Australia rather than import cheap imitations. He manufactured koala bears, kangaroos, platypus, and other kangaroo skin products in his factory at Botany and exported them around the world, predominantly to Japan and the United States.

In the early '70s, I worked in the family business for a couple of years. My role was officially personal assistant; however, I did everything from sweep the floor to pack the bears into huge boxes ready for export. No doubt some of you are thinking that koalas aren't bears. And you are right—koalas are not bears. But the Henderson family referred to 'the bears' and 'the factory' for the more than fifty years that dad was in business.

During my time in the family business, a letter came inviting dad to be part of a trade delegation going to Japan with a view to exporting Australia souvenirs. This trip was the start of the Australian Koala Bear Company exporting products to Japan for more than thirty years.

Our family home was at South Coogee, a good fifteen to twenty minute drive from the factory. Dad booked to go to Japan and then realised that I would need to drive his car to the factory and the city to do deliveries, so I had better get my driver's licence. Speed was of the essence as I only had four weeks to learn to drive his big Ford Falcon station wagon and get my licence. I was having lessons after work and would then practise on dad's car whilst driving to and from Botany.

Botany Road in those days was a single lane major arterial road groaning with the weight of heavy trucks and buses every day. The factory was located in Hickson Street, a tiny road off Botany Road, requiring a right hand turn against the traffic.

On one momentous morning as I nervously drove down Botany Road and stopped the car ready to make a quick right hand turn into Hickson Street, I missed the first break in traffic. So when the next break looked to be about to happen, I put my foot on the accelerator and took off. In the background I could hear dad saying, 'Rob, stop, stop, stop!' But it was too late. In my nervous state, I had turned the wheel to the right, but not far enough; the front left hand side of the car collided with the telegraph pole.

Traffic backed up in both directions, horns blasted, neighbours came out to see what was happening. I jumped out of the car, crying, and started to walk towards the factory, about thirty metres away. Dad jumped into the driver's seat, backed away from the pole, straightened the car up and drove it just far enough to be off

Botany Road and let the traffic flow resume, but still a distance from the factory.

'Rob, come back here. Get in the car and drive.' I thought he was crazy. Why would I do that? In my mind that was that, I was never going to drive again, never get a licence—end of story. Dad repeated his command and I stopped walking.

'I can't dad. I can't drive, I can't do that.'

'Rob, get back in the car and drive. If you don't get back in the car now, you will never learn to drive. It's okay, the car can be fixed. If you start something, you must finish it, get back in the car.'

So I did. I drove about ten kph towards the factory door, and quickly jumped out of the car. Dad didn't mention the accident all day, and he certainly didn't make a fuss of it with the other staff. That day, I had to type up some cheques that he had signed for some suppliers. There was one blank cheque for $12,000 signed ready to go. Momentarily I thought of making the cheque out to me, banking it and running away before the rest of the family found out about the car—$12,000 would last me a lifetime (this was 1971 and wages were very low). Thankfully, sanity prevailed.

That afternoon dad made me drive home and again it was a very slow trip. Just before we got home, I apologised to him for crashing the car and offered to pay for it to be fixed. He declined and repeated his message. 'Always remember Rob, whatever you start in life, you must finish. That's just the way it is.'

My father died in 1999 on the seventh anniversary of my mother's death. We clashed many times over the years, but I know that I have recalled his words many times in my personal and business life—'Whatever you start, you must always finish. That's just the way it is.'

Ricky Nowak

Ricky Nowak *is a communications expert. A highly respected and inspirational speaker, with many of Australia's top companies as clients, Ricky is a master presenter, facilitator and trainer. Her sense of style, flair and trademark good humour make her presentations entertaining and memorable. She is in great demand, especially as a catalyst for change in all aspects of workplace communication. Ricky lives in Melbourne with her husband and three daughters and her story tells us much about the priorities in her life.*

It is said, *when the student is ready the teacher appears*, and, to coin a phrase, I was that student waiting for the right teacher. In my case, the teacher was experience. And the teacher came when I least expected it, in the most unexpected place and with the most unimagined outcomes.

Let me explain. My business life is in the field of leadership and communication, working with high performing teams and individuals. It is fast-paced, innovative and one that deals with complex problems, often involving difficult people and situations—no quick-fix solutions to sometimes quick-tempered behaviours.

I am a Rotarian and I attend many luncheons where speakers bring to the platform their life's work and lessons. Three of those occasions taught me the real meaning of unconditional generosity, dedication and a passion for making a difference. This was the beginning of my learning.

Moira Kelly AO, founder of the Children First Foundation, Susan Barton AM, founder of The Lighthouse Foundation and Paul Bird, past CEO of Very Special Kids, told incredible stories, contrasting hope and despair, life and death and stories of human love and need. Their stories gave us insights into the lives of desperately sick children from the streets of third world countries, to the lives of desperately lonely children bereft of family and community, and took us into the hospice and homes of families living with children who faced life-threatening illnesses. Their work is challenging and confronting, yet all three speakers shared the same commitment to making a difference.

There were moments of truth for me during and after these speakers gave accounts of their work. The moments made me reflect on times where I had been happy to donate financially to charities or foundations rather than doing any more, moments where I didn't really think about what sort of contribution I was making and moments when I felt incredibly humble in the face of the work others were doing.

It was then that the teacher appeared and I was the student, a beginner, but eager to learn. I felt I had so much to learn, and even had something to give. I took my business card and gave it to each speaker and offered what I felt was the right contribution for me—to give of my time, expertise and heart.

I visited Moira Kelly's Farm where children are rehabilitated after life saving surgery, often handicapped but alive, and preparing to go back into their community. I worked with The Lighthouse Foundation and Very Special Kids helping them build the skills of their speakers to enable them to take their message of awareness and accountability to the community. My contribution, albeit small, gave me a sense of being able to give back – and not give up when things got tough.

How lucky am I? My children are beautiful, strong and healthy and we have been blessed with wonderful families. We are surrounded by community, work colleagues and friends who bring a great sense of balance and meaning into our lives. How lucky I am.

I wonder why it has to take a walk on the wild side of life, into the hospice, into worlds of hostility and broken hearts to make us acutely aware of how fortunate we are. In my case, this teacher helped me to look at myself and at the contribution I was really making.

Perhaps the greatest outcome was learning how much of myself I could really give. So now, when I go into the corporate world and try to find solutions to corporate problems, I know I am better equipped to give of myself than I was before.

Teachers give from the heart

Rhonda Coles

*For the past three years, **Rhonda Coles** has been a health and wellness coach, committed to giving her clients positive and practical approaches to the challenges they face. Before her current career, Rhonda had been a social worker. In this role she developed programs and managed staff working with children and families in critical need. Rhonda's story provides us with an understanding of how and why she came to dedicate herself to working with and helping others.*

In the early 1980's, I commenced a TAFE College course in Welfare Studies. I had left high school three years earlier, before completing the Higher School Certificate.

As a young adult and a mature-aged student, I had a long-term dream of becoming a social worker with a vision of working with families that have a terminally ill parent, as I had experienced during my teens. Starting a college course was the beginning of a long road to achieve a degree in social work. During my first year of study there were many challenges to adjust to, such as moving out of my family home for the first time with my son, Daniel, to a new area of Sydney, a divorce and numerous other life changes and decisions. These are all normal life events, however, they were energy consuming and at times, overwhelming.

There were a number of times during the second half of that year that I considered quitting the course as I was honest with myself that I had not put one hundred per cent effort into the time needed for study outside the classroom. I beat myself up about not living up to my own goal to become a social worker. My fear was that if I gave up, if I quit the course, I may never again give myself permission to attempt something. The voice inside me told me to keep going.

At the end of the academic year, the course coordinator, Ms. Graham, asked me to attend an appointment in her office. She was direct in saying that I had not performed well during the year and told me that I was borderline for a conceded pass. I had met the attendance requirement, however, the quality of my work and focus whilst in classes had been observed as poor. I acknowledged this, feeling totally exposed, believing up until then that I had been the only one who knew that I was not performing to my potential.

Ms. Graham challenged me with a confronting question: what was keeping me coming to college when I knew I wasn't doing at all well? She said that any other person probably would have quit the course by now. I became choked up and talked at length of my dream of becoming a social worker. Ms. Graham responded to my moment of authenticity with empathy and an embracing support. She said that she believed I was capable of more and could easily achieve my dream. Ms. Graham offered me additional guidance and support in the development of my academic written work. She referred me to the Study Skills Centre at the college to help me create a study timetable and to develop my reading techniques. I didn't look back from that moment and I have never forgotten the power of how my life moved forward from that meeting, as uncomfortable as it was for a short time.

Dr. Phillip McGraw, in his book *Self Matters*, speaks of ten defining moments and seven critical choices in life that contribute significantly to shaping the person you are today. The meeting with Ms. Graham was definitely one of my defining moments, which led me to make critical choices about my passion and commitment to an academic dream and achieving a career. Ms. Graham brought my private thoughts and fears out into the open and invited me to talk about the challenges I faced balancing study and life commitments. It served positively to reinforce my direction and the promise that I had made to myself to develop a professional career.

I have often revisited that meeting and recall how uncomfortable I felt in the moment, however, I am so grateful that it occurred. I was offered a wealth of support and discovered I was surrounded by people who believed in me. Since that time, I have completed three degree qualifications, which include a Masters degree, and I have achieved the career goals that I set for myself.

More than twenty years on, Ms. Graham and I have become old friends and maintain regular contact.

Teachers believe in you

Rachel Hawken

Rachel Hawken *was born in England. At the age of twenty-one, in search of adventure, she travelled to New Zealand where she lived for thirty-six years. In addition to her work as a librarian, she ran a business called Clearly Organised helping people with their time and space management at work and at home. In 2000, she made a sea change move to Australia, attracted by the warmer climate and ambience of Kingscliff in northern New South Wales. Here she established and still facilitates life-writing groups for Tweed Coast U3A and is a volunteer librarian for the Tweed Heads Historical Society. When you read Rachel's story you will not be surprised that her life has revolved around books and writing.*

I was an average student and a well-behaved girl at school, so the attention given to the brilliant girls and the naughty girls didn't come my way. I didn't stand out from the crowd. School teachers didn't bother with me nor did they make an impact on my life. My greatest achievement was acknowledged at Speech Day with the silver cup for Good Practical Housewifery, and this at an English Grammar School specialising in academic subjects. Mortification, indeed! Schooldays were not the best days of my life.

My favourite teacher was my dad. He taught me old-fashioned values, the things that helped me to get on in life, like tolerance and a sense of humour. He used to say, 'Do your best and leave the rest', when I became stressed about exams and tests. To discourage materialism, he said, 'You can only sleep in one bed', and to calm me down when other drivers behaved badly on the road, 'You can only drive one car'. Friends and acquaintances used to go to dad for counsel and, although he has been dead for several years, people still say to me, 'Your father was such a wise man'.

I also learnt lessons from mum. Her advice, 'Least said, soonest mended', rings in my ears as I hold my tongue and bite back hurtful and angry words I know I'll regret later. 'The onlooker sees most of the game', was another of her truisms. She believed in living by the 'Do as you would be done by' philosophy (perhaps better phrased as 'Don't do to others the things you wouldn't want done to you'). I am still grateful to her for stressing the importance of grace, courtesy and good table manners even if they are no longer appreciated in today's rude and crude society.

Above all, the most important thing my parents passed on to me is a love of reading. They introduced me to the magical world of books, the library, and what was to become, eventually, my fulfilling occupation as a librarian. I followed the career advice in the book, *What Colour is your Parachute?* 'Where do you go when you have time to spare? Think about getting a job there'. Browsing in a library was exactly where I spent my spare time and still do.

I lose myself in books. They are my constant companions and I am bereft if I haven't got one by my side. I am entertained, comforted, inspired and educated by books. There's always a book which mirrors the situations we are going through—someone has been there before, and written about it. Carol Clewlow's *Keeping the Faith* put into perspective my strict religious upbringing, as did Robbie Neal's *Sunday Best*. Margaret Forster's *Diary of an Ordinary Woman* is my favourite depiction of a woman's life during the last century and Anne Morrow Lindbergh's *Gift From the Sea* is food for thought as I walk along the beach where I live. I identify with Wendy Orr's characters, the women who marry and settle far away from their home countries, in *The House at Evelyn's Pond*. When I was going through my divorce, *Men are*

Just Desserts taught me not to make men the 'main course' in my life, but to think of them as an optional extra that might be quite pleasant to complete the 'meal'.

Mum and dad died within two years of each other, both in their eighty-seventh year. It comforts me to know that they were both happily reading, in their own home, until their last days. Dad, as many boys did in his time, left school at an early age to earn a living and thereafter educated himself by reading. He could recite poetry and Shakespeare at the drop of a hat. Mum lost herself in tender romances, family sagas and the inspirational verse of gentle women.

Literacy and a love of reading are the greatest gifts. I am rarely lonely or bored, I can always pick up a book. I meet interesting people at book clubs. Conversation is stimulated by what we read and our topics range across the full spectrum. It is significant that prisons are filled with people who cannot read well. Thank you, dad and mum.

Rachel and Teagan Cliff

Rachel and Teagan Cliff *are sisters who live in Brisbane. Teagan has just turned seven and Rachel is nine. Both girls love singing, reading and playing with their cats (one of whom, Snoopy, is a bit confused about what he is as he spends ninety per cent of his time in a frock in a pram). This year, Rachel and Teagan changed schools— a move that can sometimes be challenging. It is interesting that they both chose teachers from their new school, Patrick's Road, Ferny Hills, as their favourite teachers.*

Rachel Cliff

Miss Martinez is my favourite teacher. I overheard her telling another teacher just after I started in the new school, that I was a star student and that she was glad that she had me in her class. She spoke for what seemed like ages about how helpful I am, and how I work hard and am really smart. I felt proud inside and happy when I heard her say that.

I want to keep being a star student because she believes in me. She tells me things like 'great work Rachel' and 'that's the best work I have seen from you all year'. She constantly encourages me and the rest of the class to keep going even when it is hard. She gives us little stickers when we have done a great job, as well as homework holidays and happy grams to our parents praising us.

Miss Martinez believes that everyone in the class is special. We have had some kids leave my class and Miss Martinez threw a surprise party for them. We got to say goodbye to our friends in a special way, which made it easier because we wouldn't see them anymore.

I have learnt from Miss Martinez that if someone believes in me, then I learn to believe in myself. I can be whatever I believe I can be. I **am** a star student, even on the days when I am not so sure of that myself.

Teagan Cliff

I have the best teacher in the whole world. On my first day at my new school I felt really scared and funny in my tummy. Mr Kozak squatted down in front of me, looked me in the eyes and told me that it was his first day at that school too and he was a bit scared and funny in his tummy. I didn't know that adults got scared at times. He taught me that being scared is okay. You can tell someone about it and it doesn't feel so bad.

Sometimes kids in my class feel sad. Mr Kozak tells them that if we keep thinking sad thoughts then we will make ourselves even sadder. He says that if we are feeling sad we should change what we are thinking about and think about the good things around us or think funny thoughts. If we are still sad he does a funny dance to make us laugh. He tells us that we are in charge of what we think—only we can make ourselves feel happy or sad by what we think.

The funniest thing about Mr Kozak is how he is teaching my class to count by fives to one hundred. He does it by dancing around the room, wiggling his bottom—it is so funny and makes the class laugh for ages! I can now count all the way to one hundred by fives and back again. Maths is fun!

Peter Burke

For the past seven years, **Peter Burke** *has operated a management consultancy business. Prior to that time, Peter had a varied, but highly successful, career as a researcher, change-agent and manager in both the private and public sectors. Recently he has moved to southeast Queensland to follow the sun and seek new horizons. Peter's life and career exemplify the two lessons he attributes to Mr Le Blanc's influence—go to the heart of the matter and always take time to plan.*

What a difficult, if not impossible task! So many teachers from all walks of life, so many lessons learnt (and perhaps not so many applied as should have been).

My first thoughts turned to my impressionable school years and the amazing array of teachers who faced the daunting challenge of trying to educate a sometimes unwilling rabble. Many teachers stand out but one in particular quickly comes to mind as the one who provided lessons which, in hindsight, have guided much of my professional career.

This was Mr Le Blanc. What a great name! He never told us his first name. There was a rumour that his first name was Fred but I dismissed that immediately. How could someone so capable (and with such a great surname) have Fred as his given name?

Although I didn't realise it at the time, Mr Le Blanc had what would now be described as 'presence'. He wasn't flamboyant or gregarious. He had a dry sense of humour which rarely surfaced. He worked us hard and we responded. I guess he took us and his profession seriously. Maybe we felt we had to respond in like manner and we treated him seriously.

I learnt two extremely valuable lessons from Mr Le Blanc.

The first and most valuable lesson for me was to always seek out the essence of whatever was of interest—to find what really lay at the heart of the matter and to be able to understand for myself and where necessary, convey that essence to those that might be concerned. Unfortunately, we are enmeshed in a world where quantity and complexity reign. A world where we must seek to make our way, relate to and help others, amidst a clamour of information, much of which is untrue, irrelevant and sometimes knowingly deceitful. Mr Le Blanc provided the motivation and the tools to help me sort my way through this clamour to a view of the essence.

We must have précised every piece of English literature that was ever written, or at least it felt that way. We then had to explain the basis of our summaries. At the time it seemed like it would never end but I believe at exam time, to our very great relief, not one of us had any difficulty interpreting and understanding what the examiner was seeking.

The other extremely valuable lesson I learnt was to take the time to plan. Mr Le Blanc understood that when we faced complex tasks that had to be accomplished in set periods of time—such as exams—the immediate reaction after panic had hopefully subsided, was to get stuck into the questions as quickly as we could. He worked with us to explain and illustrate that time spent at the beginning understanding the issues and planning our responses, would ultimately produce a better result and save time at the end for revision.

He showed us that this approach could be applied to any issue where time was short, pressures significant and hot heads were holding sway. I still feel the surge of initial adrenalin, and sometimes panic, when faced with urgent and difficult tasks, but the memory of Mr Le Blanc and his wise counsel have often seen me through.

Pam Tate

Pam Tate *runs her own business, Pam Tate Print and Promotional Products, from her home. Pam has three grown-up children and she is looking forward to the imminent arrival of her first grandchild. Pam's touching story about Jo, her special neighbour, tells us that Pam will be a caring, committed and wonderful role model for any grandchild.*

My favourite teacher is my special friend, Jo. I first met Jo when we moved into our new home. Jo lived down the road with her father, Reg. That was nine years ago and Jo was then twenty-one years old. Carly and I were unpacking some items from our car when Jo arrived on her motorised scooter. My daughter Carly was in her final year of studies and was planning to go to university to study occupational therapy. Carly had always had a gift with disabled people and somehow Jo sensed it straight away. This was the beginning of a wonderful friendship and the beginning of lessons for life that Jo is still teaching us.

Jo was born with an intellectual disability and unable to walk. She was born with a defective jaw so talking and eating take a lot of effort; effort on Jo's part to be understood and effort on our part to understand her. One hand is paralysed so she has only one good hand. Yet Jo is one of the most capable people you could ever meet. She is unique. At times she is like a ten-year old; other times she could be anything between ten and sixty. She has the wisdom of someone who has lived and loved, yet she behaves with the cheekiness of a teenager. Jo is all things.

I once thought I worked out why she has never really settled into workshop life. It dawned on me that Jo prefers the company of 'normal' people because she doesn't see herself as disabled. I told her father, Reg, that I had it worked out. He said, 'I knew that years ago.'

Jo never complains. She has a happy disposition except when she decides to growl at her dad, her primary carer. Jo enjoys ten-pin bowling, a game that she is good at. One day we took Jo bowling—my teenage son, his friend and me. Just as we arrived, Jo started to take a fit. She knows when one is coming on and the drill is if she lies down and keeps quiet they usually pass within a few minutes. We were pushing her in her wheelchair, so she slipped out of the wheelchair on to the carpet to lie down. But, as it happened, the bowling alley had loud music playing and it was Jo's favourite song.

So what she did was to lie down when the spasm came on and then, as she was coming out of it, she would start dancing madly on her back to the song. Then another spasm would start, she would lie still, then dance like mad on her back again as she became alert. This went on for some time. In situations like this people give you a wide berth and we all just sat together and tried not to laugh too hard!

Jo throws her bowling ball from her wheelchair and at this same eventful excursion she accidentally threw the ball down the side lane where the attendants walk to get to the pins. When she realised what she had done she took off at full speed chasing the ball, with Ryan after her. It was the funniest sight, with me screaming at Ryan to catch her, as we weren't sure if there was a drop behind the plastic curtains at the end of the lane.

Jo has a determined streak that showed through when she was just ten years old. Her father tells a story of when Jo first learned to swim. At the swimming carnival she wanted to go in the fifty-metre race, which she did. But she wouldn't get out until she reached the other end. It took her twenty minutes to finish the race.

In the suburb where Jo lives she is known locally and she touches the lives of all those who make the time to get to know her. Their lives are enriched and they appear to go out of their way for her. Every month the local jeweller polishes her prized 'wedding ring'; the bike shop people give her caps and t-shirts; people in the street and surrounds drop in to give Jo presents at Christmas and on her birthday. Everyone is advised at least two months before that a birthday is imminent!

Jo has taught me love, patience, determination and a whole lot more.

Teachers come in many guises

Nina Hope
Tory Richards
Leanne Farmiloe

Nina Hope *has her own company which coaches small business in the financial services industry. Nina began this story and then realised she needed to incorporate the ideas and memories of her sisters.*

Tory Richards *is one of Australia's most highly regarded property executives with more than twenty years national and international experience.*

Leanne Farmiloe *gained her MBA from UQ and notes that it has been useful for the business side of her life, but no use at all for managing three rambunctious children!*

Because my family moved every couple of years and I went to nine different schools during the course of my education, I felt at a bit of a loss when confronted by this topic. How could I identify what my favourite teacher taught me when I couldn't even remember any of the teachers?

So, when in doubt, call in the troops! I contacted my two sisters for consultation about the subject, and we sat, with a bottle of Moet (any excuse!) and after much discussion we realised that the people who were cornerstones in our lives were actually those omniscient, interfering and nagging hangabouts...yep, our parents.

Always there, always watching, always disciplining and, to their minds, always right—and finally, we've had to concede that in many ways, they actually did get it right. The lessons we learned from them, sometimes painful, have helped all of us to succeed in our lives, on both a personal and financial level, and are the same lessons we are now trying to teach our own families.

Mum and dad taught us many things, but something that we accepted without question as an unequivocal force in our lives was the importance of family. Being a somewhat goal-oriented, bullet point-driven and achievement-directed bunch, we recognised that FAMILY would provide a good structure for analysis and understanding. So, here we go—

F

Faith	Have faith in yourself and in what you can do.
Fitness	Respect your physical and mental fitness. Both impact hugely on how you handle the demands life sends you.
Fun	Enjoy life and laugh a lot. Don't take things too seriously. If you ever do start to take yourself too seriously, contact a family member who will be happy to sort you out!

A

Act	Have a go! Don't be rendered inoperable by self doubt or fear.
Attitude	Maintain a positive attitude through adversity. Personal growth often occurs when the going gets tough.
Adapt	Don't be intimidated by a new environment. Work out how you can adjust to it and use it to your advantage.

M

Music
Music was an important part of our upbringing. We learnt to appreciate it, to dance to it, to recognise its importance in the rhythm of life.

Mistakes
We all make them. Always take responsibility for them, learn from them and try to turn them into positive experiences.

Moments
Enjoy the small things in life and appreciate the little memories. Sometimes they will have more significance in your life than you can predict.

I

Integrity
Always live by your integrity. Even if, on the surface, there is no immediate or obvious return, at the end of the day you have to live with yourself, and inside you will always know how you should have acted. Life has a way of returning the acts that you do.

Independence
Have faith that you can do what you want to do, and do it yourself. You don't have to rely on other people—you can do it on your own.

Ideas
We were encouraged to pursue our ideas, nothing was stupid and lateral thinking was applauded. All of our successes in life have sprung from good ideas.

L

Love	You can never get enough or give enough of it. Life is not just about money or success. Finding a life partner who will support you and give meaning to your life is an essential part of the journey. Our parents met and married young, they have always stood steadfastly by each other, never levelled criticism about each other to others, including significantly, their children, and always provided the best example of what love is about—commitment, understanding and standing united.
Level thinking	There are always temptations to get caught up in the hysteria or politics of a situation or job. Refrain from participating; all that energy is wasted on this type of negative behaviour.
Loyalty	Remain loyal to those who are important in your life. No further explanation needed.

Y

Yourself	Be yourself no matter what the circumstances. Always be true to yourself so you can look in the mirror each morning and respect the person looking back at you.

Much of the above may seem clichéd, but to us it is real and has helped to guide our success in life. Our parents must have done something right as all of us are happy, secure in whom we are and have achieved significant financial and career success. All of us hit millionaire status, independently, and in completely different work arenas, by our thirty-fifth birthdays.

As we get older we realise just how tough it was for our parents and yet, in spite of the circumstances, how steadfastly they held to the creed, one they had learnt from their parents. Stay true to the ones you love; defend at all costs. Our parents didn't have much financially as children, but the wisdom they have acquired over time has immeasurable value.

And thus it is that we feel an obligation to our own children to do our best to pass on this legacy from our favourite teachers—our parents.

Nana Yaa Larbi

Nana Yaa Larbi *from Ghana in West Africa, completed her studies to be an electrical engineer in her home country but she now lives in England with her four young sons. When we read her story we understand why Nana is now training to be a secondary mathematics teacher.*

I wish I could show him what he has helped me become.

I wish I could tell him how grateful I am for his life.
I wish I could tell him how he opened up my eyes to the beauty of Maths.
I wish I could tell him how I became respected for the new knowledge he helped me acquire.
I wish I could capture on film, for his enjoyment, the first time someone asked me to help her with a problem she couldn't solve.

I wish I could show him what grade I got for my A level.
I wish I could tell him how I topped one paper out of almost two hundred students when I started doing engineering; and mention that I was one of only four girls in that class.
I wish I could tell him some of my male colleagues in school told me they had heard about the girl who was 'so good in Maths' before I got there.
I wish I could show him how my presentations are still as neat as he taught me to write them.

I wish I could show him the Maths books I keep buying out of the love for the subject, which he deposited in me.

I wish I could ask him to teach me how to be as good a teacher as he was.

I wish I could give him something that would show my gratitude and affection for restoring a part of my self-esteem.

I wish I could honour him before the whole world and make someone grant him an award.

I wish I could tell Mr Ogbarmey-Tetteh that he was my favourite teacher.

I wish I could tell him that he was more than a teacher to me.

I wish I could tell him that he was my coach and my mentor and my redeemer at a point in my life when all around me was crumbling.

I wish I could hug him and let my tears speak for themselves.

I wish he hadn't died when he did so that he could see his legacy passed on to the children that I will be teaching.

I wish I could do all these things, and so now I teach.

Merilyn Wallace

> **Merilyn Wallace** *lives with her family on a picturesque five acre property in Bonville, near Coffs Harbour, on the beautiful New South Wales mid north coast. She is a freelance editor, writer and proofreader and runs her own home-based business called Correct Editing. Merilyn is a member of the NSW Society of Editors. In her story, Merilyn shares with us the lessons of a lifelong relationship built on trust and love.*

When I was nineteen, my favourite teacher taught me how to drive. At the time, my best friend was having driving lessons too and she often complained to me about her instructor's attitude. 'He goes off his head at every single tiny mistake,' she said. 'I get so nervous and flustered, I make more mistakes. We always end up yelling at each other.'

While I encouraged my friend to persevere, I couldn't help feeling lucky that my driving instructor wasn't like that. When I bunny-hopped his car down every street in our neighbourhood, my favourite teacher chuckled and said he'd done the same thing when he was young. When I forgot where the foot brake was, nearly knocking down a terrified pedestrian, my instructor calmly wound down his window and apologised to the poor lady on my behalf. At the end of each lesson he'd tell me my driving was 'coming along nicely, love' and that he looked forward to the next lesson. A few months later, after I'd passed my driver's test with a near perfect score, my favourite teacher let me borrow his car whenever I needed it. I even had my own set of keys.

Much earlier in my life, my favourite teacher taught me to love books. When I was a child he would entertain the whole family with hearty recitals of RL Stephenson, Enid Blyton and AA Milne. He never read with a bored, distant voice as some adults do when reading to young ones. Rather, he gave the words life and meaning, as if he was sharing with us the world's most treasured secrets. My favourite teacher's enthusiasm for books made learning to read fun and created for me a lifelong passion for the well-written word.

My favourite teacher was fanatical about Aussie Rules football and barracked for the Richmond Tigers. One night, a small child innocently stepped in front of my favourite teacher's TV screen, interrupting for only a second the Saturday night footy replay and receiving a sharp tap on her backside for doing so. I was that small child and at the time, felt insulted by such a rebuke, all over a, dare I say, silly game. A year later, I was disgusted to witness my older brother had joined ranks with my favourite teacher. The pair of them would perform the same ritual every Saturday night, gluing their eyes like zombies to the footy replay and taking absolutely no notice of me! I was determined not to fall victim to this sinister addiction, but my favourite teacher had other ideas.

Several times that season, my favourite teacher took my brother and me to the famous MCG where we sat on cold seats with thousands of other Melbournians and watched the Tigers and other VFL teams in action. At half time, my favourite teacher used cunning strategies to win me over to his 'silly game', including bribery: meat pies with lots of sauce; hot, salty chips; ice cream; and—my favourite—fruit and nut chocolate. He explained the rules of footy, told me how to read the scoreboard and how to identify the players by the numbers on their backs. He taught me the Richmond Club's victory song and, when the crowds were too big, sat me on his shoulders so I wouldn't miss a thing. By the end of that season, my resistance had so weakened that on the last Saturday in September I sat with my favourite teacher, glued my eyes to the TV screen and cheered our beloved Tigers to a grand final victory.

During my favourite teacher's remaining years, we shared many more memorable moments over Aussie Rules footy and he never forgot the fruit and nut chocolate!

My favourite teacher taught me other important things: how to love my family; how to be kind; how to be thankful for each of God's blessings; how to work hard and carry life's burdens without complaint or bitterness; how to accept others and be content with a simple, uncluttered life.

On 1 November 1999, God called my favourite teacher home. He had taught long and well. My favourite teacher is my dad and while I'm sad that he's beyond the boundaries of earth and time, I sense that his life still reaches me, speaks softly to my heart, and every day teaches me something good.

True teachers are remembered with love

Megan Tough

Megan Tough *has her own business, Action Plus, where she works with executives and managers in constructive but fun environments to develop their skills and effectiveness as leaders. Megan loves everything to do with health, food and fitness, and she has a personal mission to trek on every continent of the world. Megan's story tells of her first career trek from Perth to Sydney and the crucial lessons that she learnt from her favourite teacher.*

I didn't meet the teacher who had the biggest impact on my life until I was twenty-six years old. He was my boss for nearly two years and I did more growing in those two years than I would have thought possible.

John was a brilliant man, with large ideas and extremely high standards. He started his own IT company and set about filling it with people he believed could turn the dreams for his business into reality. I was fortunate enough to be selected, so I left my home in Perth and relocated to Sydney for one of the best adventures of my life.

I learnt three big lessons from John.

1   When you have unshakeable belief in someone else, it rubs off on them.

With nothing but his intuition to go on, John believed in me unswervingly. It didn't matter that I had no relevant experience, or that what I knew about computers would fit on the head of a pin.

He believed I could hold down responsible senior positions, and so I believed it too. Sure, I was nervous and uncomfortable, but over time I felt a growing sense of pride, and a realisation that he was right.

He believed in me so I believed in me. Without my renewed sense of self-belief, it is unlikely that I would ever have considered leaving the safety of the corporate world and starting a business of my own. Now I look for opportunities to put my faith in other people because I know first hand what a powerful support that can be. Through my coaching I get to do it everyday.

2 I am a great public speaker.

No matter who you were when you came to work in John's organisation, you were destined to leave a significantly improved presenter and speaker than when you arrived. There was no room for doubt on this one. Everyone in the company was required to give internal and external presentations on a wide variety of topics—often ones in which you had zero expertise and only a couple of days to find out what you needed to know.

In my school and university days I used to get so nervous at the thought of speaking up in groups that I literally couldn't talk in discussion sessions or tutorials. If I did manage to get up the courage, my face would turn bright red and the sweat would be pouring off my body.

John gave me no choice in the matter, so I was forced to overcome my fears. The highlight of my presenting skills came when I toured rural New South Wales giving a high-level strategy and technical presentation to corporate IT managers. I was complimented on my knowledge and style. Unbelievable! These days I actively seek speaking engagements, and being up in front of groups is one of my all time favourite activities.

3 Lessons in leadership.

I encountered inspirational leadership for the first time in this company. John wasn't always easy to get on with—his very high standards and sometimes short temper meant we were often advised of our shortcomings. But, to contrast with that, he gave us opportunities that nobody else would have, he expected us to learn things that were totally out of our current sphere of knowledge, and he believed in our abilities. He didn't want us to be pigeon-holed by our jobs. He wanted us to use our brains and extend our abilities.

Many of the things I know today about leadership, motivating others and creating brilliant cultures, I learned by watching him in action. I haven't found another work environment since that comes close to matching what we had there, nor such a dynamic individual to admire and respect as a leader.

Lizzy Malcolm

Since earning her drama degree and teaching qualification, **Lizzy Malcolm** *has spent much of the last ten years travelling and living abroad, gaining experience in marketing and honing her writing skills. She recently worked on a volunteer project in Nepal and is now based in Sydney working towards her goal of assisting aid efforts for children abroad by writing about her experiences. Her story here shows the style and magic we can expect from her future writing.*

I was feeling a little worn and sleepy after work, surrendering myself to the rhythm of the train as it lumbered closer to home. A recent addition to Sydney, I was still getting used to the city's rush and demands, but as a bright-eyed twenty-three year-old I wouldn't have been anywhere else in the world. Love had brought me here and it would keep me for many years. As we slowed to a stop that wasn't mine, I let my eyes have their way and closed them to think of the man waiting for me. The train started to move again, finally obeying the magnetism between my body and my boy, and I lifted my lashes.

Bang. My breath caught short and I bit my lip to keep from gasping aloud. My eyelids forgot one another and I couldn't make them reconcile for a moment. That person, that man there, I know him. I've never seen him before in my life but I know his bones. I felt my skin looking at him, I sensed my blood cells straining in his direction. I had never imagined a feeling like this in my life but I was breathing, this was real.

He was standing only a few feet from me, completely absorbed in a crossword. I felt frustrated at first, thinking I must have met this person before but just couldn't place it. Still, mere recognition didn't feel like this. This was extraordinary. I studied him as he pondered his puzzle and my will to remember him disappeared. I was looking at something that affected every inch of me. It was as though I had known him as long as I had existed; that everybody I had ever loved was inside him somehow. I couldn't bear to look anywhere else. I was completely transfixed and the rock of fizz in my belly was fast filling me to my edges. Fighting a rush to call out made me feel sick. Why wasn't he melting in my presence the way that I clearly was? He hadn't even seen me.

Or maybe he had.

We had reached Town Hall station and I wondered if I might actually cry. I was super-charged and glass-fragile all at the same time. As I stood, my spine sang out for him to follow me. And he did, even when I went up the steps that nobody else ever seemed to use, even when I obediently stopped at the lights to cross a quiet street. When we reached the second stop, he stood right next to me; so close I could smell his sweetness. My brain was screeching at him, 'You are the most beautiful thing I have ever seen! I've known you forever. I could love you right now.'

My lips caught each word in its rush, pausing to see if they should be freed. My heart was taking running jumps at my ribs trying to get to him, my pulse had lost control and spun wild patterns under my skin.

He followed me to the third stop and I thought my legs might buckle at any moment. His arm was touching my arm. I was going to fall. He leaned slowly toward me until his face was only a breath from mine. I will never forget that look. He was waiting. His eyes were full of questions. And all I could think of in that moment was the love waiting for me to come home; my best friend. I was trembling when I stepped away from him and immediately I felt him gone.

My favourite teacher was in his early twenties, had brown curly hair, beautiful green eyes and loved to lose himself in crosswords. I can't tell you his name or where he is from. I never heard his voice and he, in turn, never heard mine. He was in my life for the few minutes it takes to travel between Milsons Point and Town Hall stations. Yet that person will forever be the one that changed the possibilities I see in life. He taught me to believe in magic.

Teachers open doors

Lisa Dunn

Lisa Dunn *is the lucky person who lives with her husband, Trevor, and their two children on beautiful Magnetic Island in far north Queensland. Lisa and Trevor are embarking on the adventure of converting an old pineapple-packing shed into their home. Lisa is chronicling their experiences in a new book, which she hopes will encourage others to renovate. If the new book has the same verve and enthusiasm as her story here, it will be great fun to read.*

This was my very first trip to Sydney, in fact anywhere, by myself. I was all fired up. Sydney was where all the rich and famous people lived. I might even see one! Whoo Hooo. I had my hair done, bought some new clothes and even painted my fingernails. Now, that was a first! I was thinking, 'Wouldn't it be great if I got to sit next to someone on the plane who was going to the same course as me'. Well, lo and behold, I did. Amazing!

I had a window seat and I watched the sun come up through the clouds. Just awesome. It was just like being in heaven, all white and silver. As I was checking out the in-flight magazine, as you do, there, right in front of my eyes, was a photo of my beautiful children. So, there I am in the aisles waving the magazine around showing anyone who would look. A proud mother. This was just toooo excellent!

We changed planes at Brisbane airport and my feet were absolutely killing me 'cos I had chosen shoes that looked great but hurt really bad. Then I thought, 'I wonder what it would be like to be paged'. Well, no joke, it happened. They called my name over the loud speakers and asked me to go to the luggage area. Oh my gosh what had I done?

So now I was convinced I was a witch. They explained I had nail polish remover in my bag, which was not allowed and could have blown the whole plane up. Oops! Not one to waste an opportunity, I stashed the magazines into my bag and changed my shoes. Ah! That felt better. Someone was looking after me. Then back on the plane I was sitting next to my new friend again. Excellent! I had the very best weekend in Sydney. It was a ripper, but that is a whole other story.

It doesn't end there—the flight home was even more amazing. I was sitting at the airport downing my Big Mac when I heard someone say, 'Look there's Richard Branson, walking around just like the humans'.

'Hmmm', I thought. 'Wouldn't it be cool if he was on my flight?' Well, not only was he on my flight, but he sat next to me AND shook my hand AND he signed every bit of paper I could get my hands on as well as all the in-flight magazines with that photo in it, AND a copy of his book. He was very gracious and nice, but the poor bloke would have had RSI by the time I had finished with him.

This whole incredible experience has taught me that it really is true that what you focus on is what you create. What you feel is what you attract. This is proof.

Crikey, I reckon I could have manifested almost anything that weekend.

Now....to do it again.

Kylie Saunder

Eight years ago **Kylie Saunder** *joined the fitness industry having spent the previous ten years assisting senior management teams in the corporate world. Kylie now owns and runs a Pilates studio in Melbourne. Her approach to fitness and health encompasses holistic principles, and as a practitioner and presenter, Kylie is known for her special interest in spiritual health. Kylie's personal journey towards the acceptance of holistic principles is effectively illuminated in her story.*

Three years ago I received letter box advertising for a yoga class in a community hall, five minutes walk from my home. Having practised yoga on and off for ten years or so, it sparked my interest as I had never found a teacher that I gelled with. I rang the number and chatted to the teacher for about twenty minutes. She suggested I attend the class that Friday. When I entered the room I felt a warmth and positive energy. The smell of incense and the soft chanting music made me feel welcome and expectant of a new journey.

This was my first Iyengar yoga class, a style of yoga that places great importance on technique and body placement. It is perhaps the most disciplined of all the yoga practices. During the class, my mind was overwhelmed with all the directions. I felt as if my mind and body were not uniting as they should. Then the challenges really started, mentally and physically as the teacher said, 'Okay, take the mat to the wall and we'll do handstands.'

I stood still and watched the rest of the class go to the walls. Women twice my age and three times heavier than me were already performing handstands and not only performing them, but holding them for periods of one to two minutes. The teacher came over and gave me the instructions. She smiled, then said, 'Use the intent and the energy will flow. It will take you five to six weeks to do this if you practise at home four times a day. Persist, set your intention, and then detach from it. Don't do more than four times a day though.'

My first attempts were beyond dismal. I only managed to get my feet onto the wall by having the teacher lift my legs up. But, after the class I felt a sense that I had come home, that my mind and body were connected. I felt whole and eager to explore this more.

Over the next few weeks and months, I not only practised the handstands at home but attended her classes twice a week. At each class I was pushed, not only physically but mentally. It seemed as if she knew what the class needed mentally to be able to perform physically. Phrases like 'discipline in yoga, leads to freedom' and 'release the body sensations while focusing on the breathing' flowed to us while we were in the postures.

Over time, the lessons I learnt in each class started to translate into everyday life. If I felt myself becoming stressed, I remembered to breath, like in yoga when I was in a challenging posture. The more I experienced what was happening at that moment, the more I connected with people around me instead of wanting to run away. When particularly challenging times came along I used the discipline I gained from my yoga and got through them, rather than struggling and flailing.

This teacher has taught me to live in the moment and to bond with myself and others around me. She has inspired me to practise yoga daily as a way to continue the inner journey and connect with who I am.

Kerrie Akkermans

Kerrie Akkermans *is a business consultant and professional speaker. She has a Bachelor of Communication and is director of Akkermans Corporate Development as well as owner of a large retail business. Kerrie has worked with over 300 business clients helping them refine their message, develop effective customer relationships and establish strategic alliances. Kerrie's story shows us how her upbringing forged a balance and a perspective which she has successfully brought to her life and businesses.*

My father, Denis, was a teacher by profession and he had a profound effect on me, both personally and professionally. When I thought about all the things he has taught me, there seemed too many to choose from, but essentially they all came down to the one theme—perspective.

It was tough having a parent teaching at the same school that I went to. Firstly, everything that happened to other kids was my fault. Secondly, dad was harder on me because, of course, he couldn't show favouritism. Mind you, he didn't have to go so far the other way. Thirdly, do you really think any boys were going to ask me out? I don't think so!

Taking this into account, my father the teacher, still taught me many of the most important lessons I have learned in life. Perspective first became real for me when dad took my class to the airport. Now everyone thought on the way there that he was such a great guy, as he was taking us on a plane, but no, we were just going to look at them. Once again, I took a lot of flak.

What he did teach us though, is that the plane on the ground is the same as the one in the air. The position from where you see something determines the perspective you have on it. On the ground it looks huge, but in the air it looks tiny.

The view you take—your opinion—is governed by your perspective. Take mathematics, it's black and white; two plus two is four, not three or perhaps one. Now English, that's a different story. You can read one critique of a novel or film and feel you've understood it and then the next one you read has a completely different slant on it. Is one right and the other wrong? No, they can both be right. Figure that.

As my dad says, it's all about the perspective you take and the cultural and emotional baggage behind your opinion. There is always room for discussion, presentation of arguments and background research.

Consider politics: some people vote the way they do because their parents voted that way, that's the only perspective they have. Whereas other people seek out wider points of view to help form their perspective. It's amazing that siblings brought up the same way can believe such different things. I recently read *The Mitford Girls* by Mary Lovell. It's the story of six sisters growing up in England in the first half of the twentieth century. They all chose different lives—one was a socialist, one a communist, two were fascists, one a novelist and another was a peacemaker.

I was always a very good girl at school; mind you, I had to be. The only other alternative was to be very bad and that didn't fit my nature. However, one day I decided to cut the good girl image and wreak havoc along with the bad crowd by skipping school. We were caught, of course. I thought my dad would be mad, but out came another perspective lesson. When you play, play hard, but when you work, work hard.

I remember dad's lessons on perspective often when a day isn't going so well, a mishap occurs or I have a disappointment. I know it's my choice what perspective I take on it. How much will I let it affect my life? In the end it's up to you. To one person an event is a tragedy, to another, it represents an opportunity. What is a dump to some, is a palace to others.

It's all about your perspective.

Teachers show the way

Judy Mason

Judy Mason *has worked for commercial television in both Sydney and Melbourne. Since moving to the Gold Coast, she has been involved in human services and community work, especially in support of the Challenge for Cancer. Judy has been active over a number of years in the entertainment industry on the Coast, producing highly regarded variety concerts and pantomimes. Recently, she assisted the legendary Max Bygraves with his latest book, The Golden Years.*

As I think back on my school years I am saddened to confess that there are teachers' faces I can't put a name to and others that are just a blurred image. However, the mind and soul have a way of holding close the memories and people who are especially dear to one's heart. For me, those special people are my grandmother and one very patient teacher.

My mother was English and my father was born in Australia. Dad was a marine engineer in the merchant navy and married my mother in Falmouth, England in 1939. I was born in England shortly after the war. These early years after the war were not easy for our family. My father as a merchant seaman had survived physically but his harrowing experiences and the horrific deaths of his shipmates had left him emotionally scarred. In 1946 my mother, brother and myself sailed from Southhampton, England, to join my father in Australia.

I must have been a rather odd child. I had a speech impediment and apparently never ended any of my words and therefore I spoke a unique language that was the exasperation of my parents and subsequently, my kindergarten teacher. I have never been told or understood why, as a child, I had a speech impediment. Perhaps it was a result of the emotional tension in my father's life which affected all our family.

My first year at school was at Chatswood Primary School in Sydney. My school days were lonely as I was mimicked and teased by my classmates. At the time, my grandmother was a companion to a friend and for three days during the week, she stayed at her friend's home situated one street back from my school. Unbeknown to the playground teachers, I had found a way of slipping out of the schoolyard at lunchtime. I would run through the nearby park and arrive breathless to where Grandma was staying. She would always have a special treat for me and then walk me back to school. She never reprimanded me, she just understood.

Grandma was beautiful. I clearly remember her very special smile. She wore her thick, white, silky hair high on her head. Her dresses were beaded and she always wore a pinafore over them while she was cooking and working. One of her sayings was, 'It's not a sin to be poor but it's a sin to look poor'. She was a remarkable woman. She had survived two world wars, lost her three year-old daughter, a husband and a son, and at the age of eighty she embarked, on her own, on the six-week boat trip to Australia to join my father, mother, my brother and myself.

My grandmother's love for me and our little secret lunchtime rendezvous helped me through that first agonising year of school until a change came into my school life. The change was my new teacher.

It's amazing that I can recall her so vividly, even though I was only six when I knew her. She was plump and happy faced and her name was Mrs Heesh. Instead of my usual escape to Grandma's I would spend my lunch hour with Mrs Heesh who read me lines and insisted I repeat them back to her. Slowly I began to end my words and my unique language faded away. It had been replaced by the English language.

Instead of being rejected by my schoolmates I began to make friends. Then came that wonderful day that I will never forget—the day when I was chosen to play the role of Red Ridinghood in the school pantomime.

Mrs Heesh gave me the greatest gift. Through her kindness, her generosity in giving her own free time and her unyielding patience, Mrs Heesh gave me the gift of communication. I thank her with all my heart.

My grandmother's love for me, and my family, led us through those years. Her love was unconditional and she was the light in my life. I still hold her close to my heart.

Judith Campbell

*In this extract from her book, Between the Kitchen
and the Creek,* **Judith Campbell** *introduces us to
Gwen, the teacher who boarded with her family
and made a lasting impression on them all. As a
small child Judith lived on a farm in New Zealand,
later leaving to attend boarding school and then
to train as a physiotherapist. Judith lived in and
around Auckland for many years in her role as
mother and wife of a Baptist minister. She has
now retired to Nelson with her husband where she
enjoys creating unique wall hangings, painting with
watercolour and oils, and her grandchildren.*

Gwen came to Matakana, New Zealand, as a schoolteacher in the
mid-1940s, as the Infant Mistress, and very quickly became one of
the community. Her love of the outdoors and rural life, combined
with her love of painting, ensured a very warm welcome into the
homes of the many farming families and there would be few who
did not have one of her paintings in pride of place in the lounge.

Gwen taught David and Bill to read and write - 'Round and
round and round and up' – 'Policeman E makes I say aye' – and
struggled to teach Chris and me sewing. She wound the handle
on the old gramophone as she taught us folk dancing for Parents'
Day, but, best of all, a shy request, and we would have a little
watercolour painting in our autograph books a few days later. This
was treasured by so many little girls and made us feel special.

However, she entered our lives much more fully in 1949. When
Kingstons were unable to have her continue boarding there, Mother

said, 'Come and stay with us until something is sorted out,' so come she did and she stayed with us for five years. At first, we children were somewhat in awe of having a school teacher 'Miss Rew' at home, but we very quickly outgrew this and she became one of the family. She loved exploring the farm and shared many adventures with us. We would all hop into her tiny 'matchbox' car and go miles along little rough side roads, up bush tracks, out to Goat Island beach on the roughest of days, the wilder the better.

Father thought we were mad, but we loved it. I can still hear her, 'Look kids, there's a painting,' as we rounded yet another corner and beheld the wonderful views laid out at our feet. Her love of painting was infectious and always there were the paper and paints at the ready to capture another glimpse of the countryside. I used to love sitting with her and having a try myself and this sparked my love of art. We would look at the finished painting. 'But those colours aren't in that tree!'

'Yes they are. Just look!'

She was most upset when Father decided to fence off one of the lovely points on the farm and build piggeries there. 'You can't! Those lovely poplars and river.' But he did. Undaunted, over she went and sat among the pigs, painting the poplars. I wandered across a couple of hours later to see how she was getting on and spotted her looking at yet another view. Suddenly something caught my eye.

'What on earth have the pigs got?'

An agonised shriek and she flew across the paddock to where she had left her painting drying. Yes, the pigs had found it and with their newly-ringed bloodied noses were investigating their find. Barely holding back the tears, she managed to mingle the pigs' blood into the foliage of the poplars and retrieve what could have been a disaster.

A few days later we were all sitting in church and the minister started his children's talk. 'Once upon a time there was a pig, and it was a very unpopular pig...'. Our pew started to shake—Father,

Mother, Gwen and we three children could not contain ourselves as we tried to stifle our silent, uncontrollable laughter. It is the one and only time I have ever seen Father unable to retain his dignity. The poor minister carried on, somewhat bewildered, and Father explained and apologised after the service.

Gwen took over the household when little Bill was born, was always the backstop on our dish roster when someone was unable to do their turn, played cards, Pit and table tennis with us, and enriched our lives in so many ways. Her companionship must have been wonderful for Mother and they remained life-long friends. But, most of all, she opened our eyes to the beauty around us and taught us to see; something for which I will always be grateful.

The best lessons endure

Joyce Fewtrell

In many ways, **Joyce Fewtrell***, now eighty-four, mirrors the history of thousands of Australian women of her background and times. Her life's commitment has been to her husband, children, grandchildren, and great-grandchildren. Her marriage was the traditional one—for richer for poorer, in sickness and in health, till death parted them. Joyce worked as a dental nurse before her marriage and in retail later in her life. She has been active and involved in church, community and sport. She is a champion networker and she has a circle of loyal friends, now, inevitably, mostly female. Her story tells us that kindness, compassion and generosity received early can have a lasting influence in our lives.*

Growing up a child of the Depression, the second youngest of six children in a working class family, I had the great privilege of meeting a kind and loving neighbour who opened other worlds to me. She became my Fairy Godmother and Guardian Angel over many years.

Aunty Marie, as we called her, had two sons. Sadly, one died at a very tender age. The other son was in his mid-teens when I first knew her. Her one regret was that she didn't have a daughter so she really 'adopted' my younger sister and me. When I first met her I was nine years old, and my sister was six. Her husband was in partnership with his brother in a newsagency. They were much better off financially than we were. My father worked on the railways and during the depression years, his hours were cut back considerably, so there wasn't much money.

Every Christmas, Aunty Marie and her family booked a cottage at Woy Woy, by the water, for three months. My sister and I were always taken with them for our school holidays. Aunty's four nieces lived at Woy Woy so they became part of the holiday group as well. What an exciting time we had as the cottage had its own swimming baths on Brisbane Water. A big Christmas tree would be installed in the front room, which was closed off for days while it was being trimmed with beautiful decorations and wonderful gifts tied on for all.

Aunty Marie was very talented in all forms of craft, especially embroidery. Coat hangers were covered in satins and stitched flowers, handkerchief sachets were crocheted in pretty colours with ribbon inserts. I have one still after all these years. There were lots of books and games. It was so exciting for a young girl.

On other occasions, Aunty would pack a hamper and take us to Manly or Balmoral to swim, or to the Easter Show and spoil us with show bags and rides. As much as our parents loved us they could never have given us such wonderful experiences in those depression years.

At a time when most women expected their main role in life to be a homemaker, Aunty taught me so much. Everything had to be starched and ironed in those days so I learnt how to iron the seams flat on the wrong side of the garment before ironing the right side, and always to iron the wrong side of a collar first so it wouldn't wrinkle. Aunty was always beautifully groomed and she taught me the importance of style, good taste and taking care with your appearance. I still use cream every day on my elbows and heels because Aunty said they show your age. I have never forgotten her lessons. She opened a window for me to worlds I did not know existed, and she showed me another way to think about what I wanted for my life.

In my early teens we moved away from my Fairy Godmother but she always kept in touch. I grew up and married. When my first baby girl was born Aunty made me baby clothes, bootees and bunny rugs, and she knitted a beautiful baby shawl. In time, my daughter used this shawl for her two children. During my thirties, I had a long period in hospital. Aunty was there again with hand-sewn nightdresses and bed jackets to see me through. She certainly was my guardian angel.

In the 1950s she developed a heart condition. Treatment at that time was not as advanced as it is now. She was always bright and looked forward to my visits. In 1957 she collapsed and died while she was sweeping her front verandah. I was devastated as were her dear husband and nieces.

Her nieces and I still keep in touch and always remember dear Aunty for the wonderful lady she was. I am now eighty-four and even though Aunty Marie has been gone for nearly fifty years, I think of her often. I know that she has been the most inspirational and influential person I have had the pleasure of knowing. I will always treasure and remember the wonderful things she taught me and think of her with love.

Jodie Hudson

Jodie Hudson, *Confidence Specialist, is based in Sydney where she has been running her own business, Rise International™ since 2001. Jodie is a passionate, energetic and inspiring young woman with a commitment to personal development and helping people achieve the level of confidence that makes for fabulous lives. Her personal story gives us an insight into her own development and the impact of her first teacher, her mother.*

Mothers teach their daughters many things and my mother was no exception. She taught me some of the basics in life like how to tie my shoelaces, eat with a knife and fork, to say please and thank you at appropriate times and to say 'yes' instead of 'yeah'.

As I hit my teenage years she taught me much more; other things that could also be called the basics in life. I learnt how to apply liquid eyeliner without smudging, to walk in heels without wobbling and to co-ordinate my shoes with my handbag. All absolutely vital lessons... ...well, they were for a girl like me, anyway!

However, the most valuable lesson she taught me was not about fashion or manners. It was a lesson that would help me live a happy life. I was sixteen (and yes, very sweet indeed) and I had fallen desperately, heart-wrenchingly, bone-tinglingly in love. Remember that? The first time your body is overtaken with nervous energy, like a thousand butterflies launched in your stomach and when life was suddenly 'just like it is in the movies' Well, that was me. My knight in shining armour had swept me off my feet completely. He was two years my senior, had a real job and drove a real car! Life was simply wonderful.

Wonderful, that is, until the curtains closed on my romantic, movie-like life and my knight rode off into the distance with a thinner and much blonder damsel. Devastated! So, I did what any teenage girl would do. I called my best friend to tell her the horrible story of my life, lay face down on my bed for hours, and bawled.

A week later and I was still depressed. The swelling around my eyes had gone down but my mood was still bottomed out and I just wasn't getting any better. My faithful best friend phoned and mum answered. Mum yelled up the stairs to me that she was inviting me to a party that night but I quickly yelled back that it was just too soon for me to leave the house.

Minutes later my mum appeared at my bedroom door. She came in and sat next to me on my bed and calmly but convincingly said, 'I know you have been hurt, but there is only one way to mend a broken heart and you won't find it here in your bedroom. You've got to put on your favourite outfit, your best lipstick, put your hair up and wear those nice sparkly earrings that you love so much. Do whatever it takes to feel better about yourself again and then get back out there! There's nothing like a new boyfriend to get over the last!'

I thought for a moment and then looked over at her. Her expression was one of experience and her smile possessed all the nurturing and love that you see when a mother passes wisdom to her daughter. She put a comforting arm around me and said, 'Come on, I'll help you get ready.'

That night I learnt something that has helped me throughout my life, whether it be mending a broken heart or breathing life back into my battered spirit after who-knows-what. I hear my mother's voice and get up, put on my boldest lipstick, slip into my favourite high heels, wriggle into my best outfit and get back out there. Back into life with my head held high!

Because there's nothing like a new adventure to get over the last!

Joan Griffiths

> **Joan Griffiths** *and her husband, Barry, moved to the Tweed Coast some four years ago to escape the bleakness of Victorian winters. Joan, a member of the Tweed Coast U3A, is currently writing her life story, and with a twinge of disappointment suggests that her story might be of more interest to her grandchildren than to her children. Her story here is told with such personal honesty that she can be assured it will be appreciated by all, irrespective of age.*

During my primary education in the late 1940s at Ormond State School in Victoria, number 3074, I might well have been judged the naughtiest girl in school. In my first year I was often in trouble for not drinking the free milk supplied, but I hated milk, especially this milk which stood for hours, unrefrigerated and warm. I also liked to pull other girls' plaits. I knew it was wrong, but I couldn't help it. Sometimes I yanked too hard and the recipient gave me a slap in return. But I guess I deserved it. After all, I'd started the whole affair.

Grade one saw me in trouble for writing on the walls of the red brick school building. It was just a couple of white chalk cats, but I got into trouble all the same. I had to sit next to the teacher where she could keep an eye on me, and all my classmates laughed at me. But I didn't care.

My teacher's name in grade two was Mrs Redpath, a formidable matron well-versed in the art of naughty children, and in her class I was very bad. An older girl, named Pamela Brown, was often mean to me, so I made up a ditty and followed her around chanting, 'Pamela Brown went to town, with her britches upside down.'

Now this was terrible stuff indeed. It reduced poor Pamela Brown to tears. Eventually though, Pamela Brown dobbed me in to Mrs Redpath and Mrs Redpath caught me out. One day, just as I was warming to the task, Mrs Redpath stopped me in mid-chant.

'Joan Radford,' she called, 'come here at once.'

But I ran away and hid in the girls' toilets. I hid in one of the cubicles, carefully locking the door, but Mrs Redpath had seen where I'd gone and came puffing along behind me. Banging on the toilet door she insisted I come out, NOW! I weighed the pros and cons of staying put, and decided to open the door. Mrs Redpath grabbed me by the ear. She took me with her to the classroom, intending to give me six of the best across my hand with a leather strap, but every time the strap descended I pulled my hand away. I couldn't help it. I knew it was going to hurt and I was scared. So Mrs Redpath settled for six whacks around my bare legs, and that hurt like the devil too!

In grade three, I was a good girl. My teacher that year was Miss Hume and although she looked quite severe, she was nice to me. I liked Miss Hume. She was a good teacher, yet she was not my mentor. I knew one day there would be a teacher who would guide me on my way, but Miss Hume wasn't the one.

Grade four was with Miss Carter, she of youthful beauty and blonde hair. Miss Carter appreciated the compositions I wrote. She helped me with arithmetic, and taught me the rudiments of history, about explorers, kings and queens. Yet, although Miss Carter was a wonderful teacher and I was never naughty in her class, I knew she was not my mentor.

Grade five was uninspiring. I can't even remember my teacher's name. I began to despair. Was there no one who could take me to the level of achievement I wished to attain? I knew I wasn't a genius, but I needed to know so much more!

Then, in grade six, I found him. Mr Holden was his name, and it was he who opened a door in my mind that had hitherto been locked and bolted. It was he who found the way to explain to me what I needed to know. He showed me not only the how, but the why, because in my stubborn brain, unless I understood the why, I could never grasp the fundamentals of the how. Throughout my life, Mr Holden has been the only one with the key to unlock the strange nature of my brain.

At last I was able to comprehend so much that had been a mystery to me, most especially with mathematics. I passed as an honours student in his class and gained a certificate for that achievement which I value today.

Mr Holden was not just my teacher, he was my mentor.

Jo Eady

Jo Eady *has a deep commitment to the success of rural and regional Australia. It's in her blood. A regional business owner, Director of RuralScope Pty Ltd, a national management firm and General Manager of the Rural Women in Business Global Learning Centre, Jo often marvels at how big the world seemed when she was growing up on a farm and how small it is now, where one click connects you no matter where you live or work. Jo loves the silent nights on the family farm and the spirit of regional Australia and its people.*

Tingling with excitement and nerves, I waited to go on stage to sing solo at my primary school concert. I remember the words of my teacher. 'Do your best, look at the audience, smile and have fun.'

With these words ringing in my ears and dressed in a new skirt and yellow shirt, both made by my mum, and wearing a pair of beautiful second-hand knee-high white boots, I felt ten feet tall as I walked onto the stage that night. I have no doubt that this experience shaped part of my personality and this would not have happened without the positive influence of my teacher, Mr Wright.

I grew up in a very small rural community in Victoria and back then the concert was the biggest event on the school's calendar. Stony Creek Primary School had about thirty children and two teachers. There were times when six or so families made up the school numbers and there was always a fear that if the enrolments fell, it would drop back to being a one teacher, one room school.

Almost all of us travelled to school by bus from surrounding farms and I remember everyone being pleased when a family with children moved into the area. Girls played football and boys played netball as this was the only way we could make up a full team.

Mr Wright was my teacher for all seven years of my primary education and he taught my two older brothers and sisters as well. I owe a lot to my teacher, and of course to my parents, for what I have achieved in my life today and for the person I have become. I believe that we learn life-skills through our experiences as children and these experiences shape the way we see the world and influence our contributions when we are older.

I know for sure that singing, *Where can my kangaroo be?* as a ten year-old, all on my own, with butterflies in my stomach, at the school concert in the Stony Creek hall, taught me about self-confidence, believing in myself and doing my best. Most importantly, because of Mr Wright's confidence in me, I think it also gave me an 'I can do anything' attitude to life. It taught me much about team relationships and how little is achieved on your own, even if you are the person upfront. I was certainly the only one on the stage that night, but my whole school had sung that song with me in rehearsals and they had encouraged and supported my efforts to sing the best I could on the night. Today, I truly believe individuals can influence small groups and together they can change the world.

I can still recall the sense of pride I felt as the only child to sing alone at the concert. I also think that doing your best is all anyone can ever expect of you. I didn't quite hit the high note that night but everyone clapped and I felt great, and most importantly, Mr Wright and my parents were proud of me. It just shows what you can achieve when others have confidence in who you are and what you can do. As a result, I now encourage others to do things that they might not try on their own. It costs little to offer words of encouragement or support and yet it can achieve so much. We all have the ability to inspire others.

School was one big life leadership lesson for me as well as for all the other kids. Each week, Mr Wright gave us special jobs to do. We felt so important and it really instilled a sense of responsibility, both for ourselves, for others and for the greater good of our community. From being a milk, bell and bus monitor, to leading the playground clean-up team, stamping out library books, collecting the lunch orders and setting up the sports ground for interschool sports, we all had the chance to develop our leadership skills and to practise them in real life. Mr Wright provided us with the chance to learn about and experience leadership first hand.

Today, I own a management firm that provides people development services across Australia's agricultural and rural sectors. We specialise in leadership development, team management, workplace communication and project management for individuals, teams, industry organisations and businesses. Many of the skills we teach are what Mr Wright taught me. We just do it on a larger scale and with adults instead of children.

I often think how great it would be if others had had the chance to learn these important life and leadership lessons the way we did at Stony Creek Primary School. But then, there is only one Mr Wright and while he was at Stony Creek, he really couldn't have been everywhere else!

Jenni Erbel

Jenni Erbel, *with Nina Hope, is a co-director of Wealth by Design. Wealth by Design provides training, practice management and compliance solutions to the financial planning industry. Jenni has worked in the financial services industry since 1987. She lives in Brisbane with her husband, Steve, and their two children. Her story is a compelling example of the importance of self-esteem and how a teacher's belief that you can excel can be more powerful than any other factor in your success.*

I was born and raised in a small town in northern Queensland and I am the fourth of six children. My schooling was basic and I really didn't have much interest in learning, so I was a below average student. My two older brothers were duxes of the school and I was just a girl who couldn't fill their shoes. I was planning to leave school at the end of year ten and get a job as a receptionist – somewhere.

When the time came, I wrote my letters to prospective employees but never got around to sending them, so I went back to school in year eleven. This was the turning point in my life. I had two teachers who, unknowingly, gave me the secret to learning English and understanding the mystery of maths. The message that came across was so clear and simple, especially with maths. It's all about logic, solving a puzzle where there is always an answer. You just need to think about it and apply different methods to find a solution; it will always be there. With English, all I had to do was write about subjects that were of interest to my teacher.

Maths became so crystal clear that I used to spend most of my class-time helping other people. My teacher kept reinforcing that maths is easy and logical and it wasn't wishy-washy like history or English. Her expectation was that I would get a seven or a high distinction in this class, and I felt that I would let her down if I didn't, so I got a seven. I liked being given a challenge and I rose to the occasion. It's funny now how many times that happens to me as an adult and I wonder if she could see that personality streak in me all those years ago?

I started to get results in English as well, and in all of my other subjects. My confidence grew and I began to apply myself to my studies. My teachers showed more interest in me and taught me that if you become passionate about what you're learning, it makes it a lot easier to do. Gradually my marks improved and my enjoyment of the subjects improved as well.

Not only did it help my grades, but everything else improved as well—playing sport, relationships with guys and relationships with my girlfriends. I competed in the toastmaster's public speaking competition and took on some minor parts in the school plays. Whilst I didn't excel in these areas, the confidence just to give them a go was primarily because of this teacher. Her attitude was, 'Come on, give it a go, it will be fun,' and generally she was right. My grades went from below average to high distinctions and I was dux of the school in grade twelve and the sportswoman of the year as well. I became a more confident person because I started to believe in myself.

Fast-forward twenty years. I now hold a Bachelor of Accounting, Bachelor of Commerce, Diploma of Education, Diploma of Financial Planning and I've just finished a Masters in Financial Planning. I have applied this knowledge to build and sell my own business, which resulted in me becoming a millionaire by the age thirty-five. And I haven't finished yet!

It scares me to think of what my life would have been like if those two women hadn't taken some interest in me. They were the key reason for my success, and to them, they were probably just doing their job.

Teachers—what they do is so important. Their work should never be underrated or dismissed.

I salute you.

Teachers create options

Jason Lea

Jason Lea, *the Chocolate Man, was born into a family of chocolate makers. He worked in all aspects of the family business until he became Managing Director. After seventeen years in this role, Jason 'fired' himself and moved on to become the company's roving ambassador. Jason's story encourages us to learn from all of life's experiences.*

What a wonderful visit down memory lane. Thinking about teachers conjures up a myriad of situations and fond remembrances. Consequently, as it's impossible for me to nominate a favourite teacher, I'll present a collage.

- Mother Aloysius at an all girls' convent school that contained four ring-in four year-old boys and my most vivid memory was learning how to tie my shoelaces. I've never forgotten.
- Being taught how to lick your hand and then rub it on a well-worn varnished desk to make a squeaking sound and then announcing to Miss Brown, 'There's a birdie somewhere in the classroom,' and the understanding look received from a teacher who knew all about five year-old boys in first class.
- Becoming a cub and being taught by the cub mistress that night time is exactly the same as daytime and so nothing to be frightened of. 'Just imagine you're walking to the scout hall in the middle of the day rather than eight o'clock at night.' A lesson I've never forgotten.

- Being the eldest of seven children, responsibility was automatically shouldered, but being elected form captain and having a wonderful teacher explain to me the responsibilities of that position at twelve years of age really drove the point home.

It's interesting that none of the above, and none of the following, has anything to do with academia. It's all to do with life sciences, which when boiled down, are the only things that count. With that in mind, the brain cells start to fizz with other memories.

- For instance, how to hypnotise a chook in a chook house using a stick to draw a line in front of laying chooks. Crazy, ridiculous, but I've never forgotten it. I must admit it's been of very little use.
- Studying the moon through heavy-duty binoculars opened up another world and fascinated me for many years. Later, discovering girls, winning football games, and the pain and anguish of sitting through exams and then passing those exams and being accused by your father of bribing the teachers!
- As a seventeen year-old arriving ten minutes late to a business meeting in a solicitor's office and being chastised by the solicitor about the importance of punctuality, and it's for that reason that my watch is always set ten minutes ahead of where it should be and I have had a few birthdays since then.
- From a departed uncle the importance of detail in retail and that people really do see lots of little things.

Taking the best attributes from my parents and uncles and aunties and ignoring their bad ones and then trying to use those attributes in later life was one of the greatest lessons and gave me an all-round perspective.

Brain food is an extremely interesting phenomenon. I have learnt that water, food and air are all taken into the body and then expelled in one form or another and you're left with tiny trace elements that keep the motor going. It's the same with brain food. Words of wisdom from coaches, mentors, peers, business associates, can often slide through to the keeper. But some of them dig in. They sub-consciously become indelible and are remembered many years later.

- The best way of doing something has not yet been discovered. So please continue to stretch yourself.
- Favour received is debt incurred.
- Don't expect, inspect.
- Poor people need cheap prices, rich people love them.
- An eyeful is better than an earful. That's why TV advertising works so well.

This little list of pearls of wisdom just keeps going but I think we have run out of time. I have indulged myself by being allowed to pen the above and wish the reader well.

Jack Fraenkel

Jack Fraenkel *owns and operates Motivatories Pty Ltd, a franchise and people development consultancy, with offices in Sydney and Edinburgh. Drawing on his extensive knowledge of retailing and customer service Jack is a frequent contributor to a range of business publications. Jack's story is about integrity and wisdom—lessons for life and business he learnt from his dad.*

My dad, a very wise old German Jewish businessman, drilled into me when I worked for him in the sixties in Scotland, that the only way to build a successful business was through integrity and wisdom. For dad, both in private and business life, integrity was his sole measure of the people he interacted with. For him, integrity meant keeping your word—no matter what. In business, this means that if you make a commitment to a customer, team member or supplier, then your word is your bond—no matter what, you must, repeat MUST, keep your word!

This means that if you have told a customer that you will supply by a specific date, then, no matter what, that is what you will do. If you have promised a team member time off, an incentive, or any additional training, then, no matter what happens in your business, you must meet that commitment. If you have told a supplier that you will purchase a given amount of merchandise, then, that is what you will do. In fact, Karl Fraenkel, my dad, would have kept his word even to the point of driving his business to bankruptcy.

You see, he had adopted the current, trendy philosophy of under-promise and over-deliver long before management consultants and gurus had even thought of the term. Here's a graphic illustration of how being slightly better than your competitor at actual service delivery but not meeting your commitment as well as they do, can impact on your business.

Some years ago Citibank proposed that anyone who called them with a request prior to 9 am would receive a response by midday. Federal Bank, in the spirit of sensible competition also proposed to respond to their customers who called prior to 9 am, but not until 5 pm. This seemed to be a less responsive service than Citibank's offer.

However, Citibank dealt with their callers by 3 pm, which was three hours later than their proposed response time of midday. On the other hand, Federal Bank got back to their callers by 4 pm, which was one hour earlier than they had promised. Even though Citibank was responding sooner than their competitor, they lost credibility because their customers believed that they were three hours late. Federal Bank, on the other hand, was seen to be providing a better than expected service because they returned their calls an hour earlier than their promised time.

Even though in terms of performance, Citibank dealt with callers an hour better than the Federal Bank, Citibank experienced the worst share slide in its history, while the Federal Bank's share price rose exponentially.

So here's how integrity has helped me build my career and my business since 1967 when dad drilled into me his life lesson. Having worked in retail for most of my life, I have been at the coalface of customer interaction and staff needs. Long before legislation existed to protect consumers from a raft of perceived caveat emptor danger areas, I understood that to earn customer loyalty meant ensuring that they, my customers, were always delighted by their business interactions with me and the businesses that I managed.

I also understood, clearly from dad's input, that if my team members needed the support of, or even felt the need to consult, a trade union then I was not keeping my word and creating a safe and rewarding environment for them to work in. From my every interaction with them, my suppliers knew that I considered them as partners in my business growth as well as in theirs.

Some years ago I was managing the duty free stores at Perth airport and we supplied the wrong film to a customer. She had ordered and paid for eight reels of thirty-six exposure films but received eight reels of twenty-four exposures in error. The customer only discovered our mistake when she arrived in Nairobi where she was taking the photographic safari of a lifetime. Needless to say, she was a little upset at having to pay much higher prices for additional film whilst there.

On her return she wrote to us to outline in no uncertain terms our error and its impact on her. Our response was immediate. We sent her, by express courier, a letter of apology and thanks for identifying a flaw in our system, a cheque in full refund of the films, and her eight thirty-six exposure films which she should have received in the first place. This customer was so delighted by our response that she immediately became a raving fan who continued to refer many new customers to us over a number of years.

Survey after survey has shown that the public trust fire-fighters, pilots and nurses and don't trust marketers, salespeople, and journalists. Could the missing link for establishing trust simply be the perceived integrity at both ends of this scale? We all know that when our house is on fire, our fire-fighters will do everything in their power to save our house. My dad's customers, employees and suppliers had that same faith in him and his business. I've spent my life, to date, trying to live up to his standard, and my intention is to continue in this way.

I haven't explained to you yet, my dad's definition of wisdom. This can be summed up very succinctly, and I'll use his exact words: 'Don't make stupid bloody promises that will bankrupt you!'

———————— ⌘ ————————

Teachers teach lessons for life

Gerard Byrne

Gerard Byrne is a graduate of James Cook University, an Honorary Ambassador for North Queensland and is Manager of Communication and Information for Queensland's Department of Primary Industries and Fisheries. Gerard is known as the Grants Guru because of his passion for writing, and training other people to write, successful grants' applications. In his story, Gerard acknowledges his English teacher, Jack, as an important source of his lifelong interest in writing and literature.

Chatting to an old school mate who was in town this week started me thinking. We had spoken of friends, of fun, and the teachers we remembered. How time and circumstance does colour the memory! We both thought of Jack. Jack was one of our senior-school teachers, especially English. He struck us as a very austere and reserved man, but when we talked about him, we realised how much we both owed him.

How was Jack different? He obviously loved English. Something we, as teenage boys, could not quite understand. It was only in later life we realised how important it was to develop good writing skills, to read carefully, and speak with confidence.

We laughed as we thought how diligently Jack had laboured over teaching us the rudiments of grammar, comprehension and literature. We now know how important those English exercises were, though in the middle of summer they tested all our patience.

But Jack persevered with a dedication that has inspired me ever since. The English results at the end of term were his reward. Even he was pleasantly surprised, I suspect, but our parents were more surprised. Gone was the austerity and reservation at the start of term, as he shared in our successes at the end of the year. I remember always his smile on that day.

The memory that has lingered into adult life is how important it is to get it right, to practise, to learn, to be patient, and to share with others. I have had many opportunities since then, when things got tough, to give up. But I think back on how calmly, and valiantly, Jack persevered with us, and I have achieved my own successes as a result.

I went on to really enjoy reading. On leaving school, I even did a course on speed-reading, which helped me read more, and understand better what I had read, from the classics to Jon Cleary, Thomas Kenneally and Graham Greene. A rich world I have enjoyed for a lifetime because a dedicated, caring teacher was there to guide me, one very hot, summer in high school.

We never knew his real name. We always remembered him as Jack because he was so tall, and early in the piece, a wag had nicknamed him Jack, as in Jack in the Beanstalk. But Jack taught us the true value of always learning, and we never forgot the lesson.

Gary Summers

Gary Summers *is a widely experienced business systems expert who provides strategic advice to public and private organisations on all aspects of operational risk management. Gary has more than thirty years experience in training and development having worked with construction companies, multinationals, the tourism industry, and telecommunications companies among others. Gary's story is a frank and personal account of how a special teacher at the right time, can change the whole direction of our life.*

People say everyone experiences a midlife crisis. That may be true. What is most interesting about people and life experiences is that not everyone describes or remembers their midlife crisis. It seems that some people exist in crisis all the time. Others simply get on with life, retain a positive attitude and approach life happily and proactively.

I had a midlife crisis several years ago. It was triggered by the sudden and unexpected passing of my mother. This traumatic event affected me in ways which I had never imagined. I lost more than my mother—I lost a best friend and then I lost my way, lost my health and my income. That put severe strain on my relationship. I was at a very low point in life. I did not understand grieving.

It was during this period when I was introduced to W Mitchell by a friend who gave me a copy of his audio tape. Wow! What an inspirational effect that had on me. Hearing Mitchell's story really put my life and my issues into perspective. I was truly inspired. I walked and listened to his tape repeatedly. I heard and absorbed his message of 'It's not what happens to you...it's what you do about it.'

From that inspiration I was able to start my own recovery. Sadly, I was not able to hold my relationship together which added to my pressures, yet I was able to plan and act positively to recover. I eventually regained my self-esteem, improved my health, learned an enormous amount and grew along the way. Most importantly, I got back on track.

The improvement process led me to gain a major corporate project role with Qantas Airways in 2000. This was just what I needed, some focus and direction again. The role challenged and stretched me professionally and called up all my skills and abilities. The work required that I conduct many workshops, strategic planning sessions, training sessions and other meetings.

I was in front of many people at all levels of business. I then joined the National Speakers Association of Australia (NSAA). This provided me with a new network of wonderful, caring, supportive and successful experts from a wide variety of disciplines. I attended my first National Conference in Adelaide and registered. When I registered, they gave me a 'First Timer' pink ribbon that I wore below my name badge. As I stood in the Adelaide Hilton Hotel, the first member to approach me was W Mitchell. His very warm welcome and the wisdom and advice he shared with me in a short ten-minute talk were inspirational. Meeting him had a great impact on me. I committed to be the very best I could and to become a speaker in my chosen fields. I continued working with Qantas and the project was a major success in many ways.

I went to my second National Speakers' convention in Sydney where I actually heard Mitchell present to more than 300 speakers from around the globe. What a speaker. I joined the standing ovation and stood in absolute awe at the love and respect that the entire room showed to Mitchell.

Very recently, at my local NSAA Chapter meeting I was invited to speak to members. Who should be visiting from America but W Mitchell? At the same meeting we also heard from Shelley Taylor-Smith, Sherry Clewlow and Scott Friedman the current President from NSA in America. What a group to be part of. When I sat down beside Mitchell he was very complimentary and offered me some advice on how I might improve my presentation. What valuable advice he gave me. What an impact this person has had, and continues to have on me. So what have I learned from Mitchell?

- It's not what happens to me...it's what I do about it.
- It's up to me to take personal responsibility and fix my life.
- I must learn and apply my own coping skills for my own issues.
- The human spirit is full of passion. Learn what my passion is, harness it and use it.
- Focus on the positive outcomes of change. Don't dwell on negatives.
- Understand and follow my own inner strengths.
- Don't think like an average person.
- Realise that my life is what I decide it is.
- Change what happens in my head and the universe changes.
- Whatever I want I can achieve.

These wise words can help any person to fulfil their own dreams.

If you are not familiar with W. Mitchell's story look up his website at www.wmitchell.com

Duff Watkins

Duff Watkins *is Asia/South Pacific Director of the Cornerstone International Group, consultants to boards and management. He is a Governor of the American Chamber of Commerce in Australia and President of the Yale Club. Having read his glowing tribute to his English teacher, Miss Travis, we are not surprised that he still reads Shakespeare or that he writes with such clarity and style.*

Famous author James Michener once declined a dinner invitation with a US President in order to attend the retirement party of his high school English teacher.

'Presidents come and go,' he said, 'but truly great English teachers come along once in a lifetime.'

He was right. Mrs. Travis proved it. To say that Betsy Travis taught English literature is like saying that a shark eats. Somehow, it doesn't quite capture the intensity of the experience. At the age of fourteen we not only studied Shakespeare, we acted it. I was Caliban in the Tempest. We memorised sonnets and constructed models of the Globe Theatre, where the Bard's works were originally performed.

We didn't just read. We wrestled with Beowulf, sailed with Ulysses, and trekked through Dante's Inferno. No passive learning allowed. We memorised the Declaration of Independence, then recited it in class. For extra credit, one girl memorised and recited the entire US Constitution!

Our class performed Dickens's Christmas Carol for the whole school, earning me, made up as Scrooge, a front-page photo in the local newspaper. This was heady stuff for a bunch of rural kids living on tobacco road in a small town in the American south.

Mrs Travis taught us not only to spell but made us learn the etymology of words. Fifteen years later I passed my Latin proficiency test in university because of it. Now, forty years later, I still double check the origin of words when I write, lest I use expect when I really mean anticipate.

I moved to Australia long ago but fate allowed me to be in my hometown when Mrs. Travis retired. Though unable to attend her farewell party, I called her up and paid my respects. As a gift, her former students presented her with an airplane ticket to England and a Shakespearean Tour holiday package that included a visit to the legendary Globe theatre.

It made perfect sense.

She stirred us from our provincial ways and shoved us into the world of great literature. She took us out of our little world and into a much bigger one. She gave us the globe, so, years later, we returned the favour and gave it right back to her.

Still, I think we got the best end of the deal.

Cheryl Norkus

Cheryl Norkus *grew up on a rural property at Denison, some fifteen kilometres from Sale, Victoria. After her schooling at St Anne's College and Gippsland Grammar she worked as a legal secretary in the Sale area. Since 1996, Cheryl has worked as electorate officer for a Member of the Victorian State Parliament. Cheryl has contributed a very personal story that confirms the power of positive reinforcement.*

I grew up in an isolated rural community, an overweight primary school child with low self-esteem. The battle to leave all that behind me is ongoing. I remember feelings of worthlessness and of being unloved. My parents, who provided me with a comfortable lifestyle and an excellent education, seemed to lack the ability to show love and encouragement. I met their expectations, although I received no recognition of this.

Enrolling at a private girls' school was a turning point for me. Mrs Davies, a quintessential English lady, was my class teacher during my first year. Although I did not realise it at the time she pushed me to participate, and with encouragement, to believe that I could succeed. My years at the school lead me to much success and, although my parents, for whatever reason, did not acknowledge that success, I was extremely pleased with my endeavours. I now look back and know I could have achieved even more.

At a conference in late 2004 one speaker in particular painted a picture of what could have been my life. To hear it from someone else was confronting but also comforting. I now know others have similar feelings and beliefs and that mine were not just a figment of my imagination. I was encouraged by her words. I knew I had done the right thing in making some recent difficult decisions. I was following what felt right for me. It gave me the confidence to continue in that direction. It also showed me the importance of taking a moment, confiding in nature in whatever form you enjoy most and doing what gives you the most pleasure.

I realise I can't live the life others believe I should because it makes them feel comfortable. I want more. I want my life to have meaning. I need to feel satisfied that I have stepped out of my comfort zone and achieved my very best.

Mrs Davies instilled in me a belief that I could succeed and with the support of friends, I know I will.

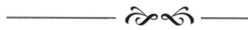

Teachers encourage

Cherie Woolven

Cherie Woolven *has had a varied career. She has worked as a receptionist, courtesy driver, company secretary, real estate salesperson and manager, business studies lecturer, job search trainer, career counsellor and life coach. Cherie is currently active in the last three mentioned. The story Cherie has written for us is a warm recollection of a very special primary school teacher.*

In the summer of 1950, at Clare Primary School, Miss Lizzie Noble introduced me to education, learning and discipline. Lizzie lived near Sevenhill, about ten minutes from school. She used to ride her motorised cycle with a knotted string skirt protector on the back wheel. She would strap her leather briefcase to the pack-rack, and was to be seen, rain, hail or shine, at exactly the same time every day.

There were many pupils, and it was our first year away from parents and siblings. It was hard to begin, but Miss Noble seemed to have a way to put us all at ease. What I remember in particular was the way in which she integrated learning with fun. She was a lover of nature and insects, and she punctuated our classes with samples of beetles, butterflies, praying mantis, spiders and other goodies. Her collection of wild flowers would have rivalled a botanical museum! She taught us to respect nature and to marvel at the wonder of it.

I recall a school play when I was to represent a cinnamon tree by holding a cinnamon stick, which I duly ate. Rather than scolding me she laughed and gave me another!

Years later my husband and I went to Clare for a holiday, and we stayed in a bed and breakfast place called *The Miss Nobles Cottage.* There were three sisters, Lizzie, Rosy and I forget the third, but relics of their days together were to be found in the cottage, including, I am sure, the very same leather briefcase that Lizzie used to carry her special cargo to school.

I wonder how many she taught in her time? I'm sure we all owe her much.

Chadia Gedeon

The year that **Chadia Gedeon** migrated to Australia from Lebanon, 1988, her first 180 minute film, co-produced with her late husband, Andre Gedeon, was screened in the Francophone Films Festival in Paris. Currently Chadia is a foreign correspondent for a cable television station in Dubai, a pre-employment trainer, a bilingual teacher of Arabic at UNSW Institute of Languages and vice-president of a Montessori school. Chadia is the founder of a new television and film production company in Sydney, called AKMAAR. The acute awareness of sensory detail in her story helps us understand why Chadia is an acclaimed filmmaker.

I was eleven years old when my father passed away. It was a hot and humid Wednesday. The night before, dad had left a new silver watch with my mother as a present for me for my first School Certificate.

Our house in Beirut had just been painted and I can still vividly recall the smell of fresh paint. Sometimes, smells can invade your senses so that even in a different place, at another time, a particular smell can take you back and link you like an umbilical cord to your earlier feelings. There was a corridor in a long L shape. My grandmother, Marie, occupied the first room in this shape. All night she used to walk up and down seeking her direction to the toilet. Her footsteps, slow and rhythmic, used to wake me up, as I was in the room next to her destination.

The day father died grandmother was very unsettled. She banged the door of each room with her stick and asked God for more patience. No-one from the family told her about the death. Grandfather was on the phone all day calling members of the family, repeating as a machine recorder, 'My son, Antoine, passed away yesterday morning. The funeral is on Sunday'.

I was waiting for my friend's father to pick me up at the examination place, west of Beirut. This Wednesday I did not return home. I had dinner with the Sisters in the convent. They tried to cheer me up with some stories of children who had grown up without knowing their immediate family. The silence in my heart was bigger than my dream of breaking these walls and going to the room where I imagined my father was lying.

The evening before he left us he called me to his room and with his feeble voice wished me good luck with the examination. His cold hands could not reach me. His eyes scrolled down and stopped at my little hands trying to reach out to his. I leaned back; the two bottles of oxygen held me tight as a cold feeling penetrated my veins. If eyes can emit sounds, a shattering sound of a massive block of glass was the language of his eyes when I turned back to look at him as I left the room. That was the last time I saw those intense eyes, soundless, and yet resonating each time I close mine.

That was thirty-five years ago.

His departure has not left me. I have lived with it since. Life has become a gradual game of hide and seek; a certain form of communication with its specific language; a definite smell of an abandoned shore. It is not the silence itself. Silence bears life within its modulations. Silence has its own language, its own musicality, its own softness and its own warmth.

Death is continuous; it is the presence of emptiness. The unknown, yet known, with all its shades and its darkness. It is slow. It is fast. It is expected and yet takes you by surprise. Nothing is predestined; there is nothing that cannot be avoided. If there are matters hidden by the gods you need only remember.

Five years now, and my brother, Roger, has been trying to live with his cancer. He turned fifty-five last June. 'Yes, another cancer in the family,' says mum, and closes her heart. Who knows better than she the long nights and the disruptive natural forces when events are totally beyond our control. Again, the fabric of what she previously knew as her reality, her security, was stripped away by the onset of uncontrollable powers beyond her understanding. Again, everything she had taken for granted was being challenged.

Today she has been told a special needle may cure her son. A needle that is so specific that it needs to be administered immediately as it contains radiation that targets only the cancerous cells. Here is another ingredient on her plate. Another hope that requires her inner strength.

'Do not be dismayed,' she hears herself murmuring in the wide silence of her early morning while she is preparing his meals. Another month to go, another night to face with courage. It is only a needle, a small needle that may change her life. A needle that will cross seas, mountains, and valleys. A needle, that, if it had existed earlier, could have changed the direction of her life.

It is eight weeks now and mum is still waiting for the needle. A needle that could prolong the life of my brother; her son. A needle that has become the centre of her multiple lives. A needle that taught her when the well is clogged, this is the right time to start cleaning. The needle that will free her to become more truly the person she is.

This is my mum, my father and my brother who all taught me to be prepared for the will of Heaven with calmness and certainty.

Celeste Kirby-Brown

> **Celeste Kirby-Brown** *has never listened to people telling her that she can't do things. As a result, she has had a successful career in sales and recruitment and now has her own career support and recruitment business. She plans to finish her Masters in Law very soon and is currently President of Women in Finance in New South Wales. Her husband and many friends support her and make sure she finds time to laugh.*

I have to admit that the idea of a friends' audit came to me one day when I was thinking about what happens with friends. Friends come in and out of our lives but the process of them going out of our lives was what had caught my attention on that particular day. I had a friend who I had been quite close to over the last year or so. We had chatted on the phone every week, and made time to see each other even though we lived on different sides of the city. Then, over a number of months we didn't call each other as often. The get-togethers became less frequent until, all of a sudden, we didn't call each other at all.

My theory on this is for that point in our lives there was something that we both needed and could give to each other. That need then passed and our friendship was still there but no longer as important to each of us as it had been over the past year. You may have experienced this yourself with your friends. That inexplicable growing apart that can happen to even the best of friends.

This process is something that I now do consciously in my life and I call it the friends' audit. Don't worry most of my friends know about this, are totally shocked and appalled, and then just laugh and accept it! It has even become a big joke with some of them—and yes, Zoe, you get an automatic pass through the next one for telling me that I should write about it!

Okay, don't get me wrong, this isn't something that I do and then ring people and say, 'You're out!' What I do is undertake a process of reflection where I try to be honest with myself and consider what I am getting out of my relationships with my friends. I ask myself if they are still working for me. Do I feel loved, supported and appreciated? Or am I the one who is constantly doing the friendship work?

Most of the time the answer will be there already. The normal cycle of not ringing each other as much or not seeing each other would already have started. I might feel annoyed or frustrated about a relationship and not know why. If this is the case and I really don't want to say goodbye to the friendship, then this period of honesty and reflection about the relationship gives me the chance to do some work on it. I can talk to my friend about it or put some extra effort into it. Or, if I think it's had its day, I recognise it, accept it and move on.

What might surprise those of you who are shocked and appalled at my idea of a friends' audit is that it also makes me very grateful for those amazing friends that I do have in my life. I take the time to recognise how much they mean to me and how important they are, and yes, sometimes I even tell them this.

The other great thing about this process is that I have room in my life for new friends. Many people seem to have the same friends for most of their lives. Great if this works for you but I believe that this may mean you shut yourself off to meeting new people who could enrich your life in some amazing way. One of my friends told me that I seem to have a constant flow of new people in my life. She is right. I know that I do and I feel enriched and refreshed because of it.

Cat Matson

Cat Matson *is a facilitator, coach and author with a zest for life and a passion for helping people get more of what they want from life. Working with small business owners for the past ten years, Cat assists them create more profit and growth and reduce stress at the same time. Cat is married with one child (so far) and she lives in Samford Valley just outside Brisbane. She loves spending time with her family, reading and walking on the beach.*

What my favourite teacher taught me was that it's important to march to your own drum—regardless of the beat being played around you.

Mr B was my year nine home-room and geography teacher—a male, controversial for his ideas and approach, not his gender, in a traditional private girl's school. He also coached my debating team, encouraging us to develop and form opinions for ourselves, and then argue them. I'm convinced that what I learnt in that year of debating is what enables me to deliver strong arguments in my business presentations today.

Mr B verged on being a hippy geography teacher, determined to save the world by planting trees, reducing his, and our, personal consumption and non-recyclable waste, and preventing multi-national companies from exploiting the environment and the people of developing nations. He was determined to save us, his students, by ensuring we understood the value of eating healthy, wholesome food. I'll never forget the story he told, with graphic detail, of his father's battle with bowel cancer and the importance of constant learning and personal development.

He photocopied the first chapter from M. Scott Peck's *A Road Less Traveled* and insisted we read it and consider how it applied in our lives. In a school that largely focused on the 3 Rs, his approach was refreshing and enlightening and through him I learned that the essence of being human is to nurture your body, environment, loved ones and most importantly, your soul.

I was in year nine at roughly the same time as the movie *Dead Poets' Society* was released, and I remember seeing the movie thinking how similar, in his differences, Robin William's character was to Mr B. In the movie, that difference cost the revolutionary teacher his job. At the time, I naively thought that such an injustice—removing the people who stand out from an often otherwise vanilla education system—could never happen in this day and age, particularly not in our school.

However, rumours flew at the end of his first and only year at our school when he announced he was leaving after such a short time. I will never know whether the pressure for Mr B to conform to my school's traditional ways was the reason he left or whether or not he was asked, ever so politely, to leave.

So, the final lesson I learned from him, intentional or otherwise, was it's often tough to be different from the crowd. Despite the pressures to be like everyone else, it's important to play your own game, to march to your own beat and to leave the world in a better state than you found it.

Bronwen Campbell

Bronwen Campbell *knows the temptation of trying to do too much. Bronwen's life is full to the brim with four young children, a husband, full time work as an Engineering IT Solutions consultant in Melbourne, a sideline training business and a macadamia farm in northern New South Wales. Add to this a desire to enhance her public speaking skills and it is no surprise that Bronwen regularly has to watch for signs of overdoing it, and work out smarter ways to achieve. With her can-do attitude, Bronwen loves nothing better than to improve her approach to life and business and to be regarded as an inspiration to others. Perhaps she learnt all about that extra stretch from an influential teacher she met at university.*

A score of six and a half out of ten! I was horrified. Maths was my strong point and I was sure that I had done everything right in this first assignment for Financial Management. My fellow students were equally unhappy with their scores, but closer investigation showed that though harsh, it was fair. We determined not to let it happen again and reviewing Financial Management assignments became top priority in the weekly MBA syndicate meetings. Our results improved, and it was clear from his approach that our lecturer had our best interests at heart, and was not there just to catch us out doing the wrong thing.

Three years later, when I no longer had Gerry as a lecturer, I submitted my draft thesis to my supervisor. He returned it with very few requirements for reworking. I should have been happy, but it just didn't feel right. I knew the work was not up to standard, but I wasn't sure how to improve it. So back to Gerry.

I went into his office, and could see the work piled up, literally, and I wondered whether I could ask him the favour of looking over my work. Did I really want this? I had just about had enough of studying for my MBA with two small children and working fulltime. With the light at the end of the tunnel, it would have been easier to just make the few minor amendments needed and walk away from it all. But I couldn't do it. Not only was it a question of my own pride, it was also the potential impact of the study itself. My thesis was a business plan for a real business and I wanted to get it right.

Gerry hardly hesitated. Of course he would look it over for me. And he sure did! It came back with notes scrawled all over it and a recommendation to completely restructure my approach. A whole rewrite! What had I done? Well, I had asked for it, so I could hardly ignore it. I knuckled down and the result was far superior to my previous attempt.

A few years later, I tried to get hold of Gerry again. 'I'm sorry, haven't you heard?' came the response from reception. 'Gerry passed away last year.'

I was so sorry—and angry! What a waste! He had so much to give and was so willing to give, and he'd been snatched away much too soon. Then I felt guilty. Was it students like me, who asked for that bit extra, for him to go that extra mile, who made him neglect his own health? Maybe if he had had more time to look after himself. I don't really know if it would have made any difference, but I always wonder.

I remember my mother saying to me when I had my first child, 'Once you are a mother, the most important person to look after is yourself. Without you, everything falls apart.' And it is so true. I can't afford to get sick, there are too many people relying on me. It is immediate and obvious when you have children; a day off sick and the cracks start to show, two days, and things can become total chaos. Even letting yourself get overtired can have a detrimental effect on the general wellbeing of the household.

It is much more subtle in other situations. Whether it is trying to be conscientious and do the right thing by your employer, your clients, or your students, or whether you like helping people and find it hard to say no, it is easy to find ourselves working too hard. We drive ourselves into the ground and all too often it is our health that suffers.

Gerry taught me the tremendous value of going that extra mile. He got results from me that others would not have known I was capable of. But, quite unintentionally, he also taught me that to be most effective, we have to look after ourselves as our number one priority. To overdo it, is like being a shooting star; your light will shine brightly and people will notice, but it is over all too quickly. You can still be a star, but not one that is burnt out. Ask for help when you need it, use your network, allow yourself to say no, refer people to others, or delegate, and recognise the signs that you are pushing yourself too hard. Then DO something about it.

So what did I learn from Gerry? The impact you can have on other people when you go that extra mile. And what else? The loss to other people that comes from burning yourself out.

If you really want to help others, look after yourself first.

Barbara Gabogrecan

When **Barbara Gabogrecan** *decided to leave teaching she established an art business and in its second year she won seven of the Australian Gift of the Year Awards with her silk product. Not satisfied with that, Barbara moved on to develop a Micro Business Network, a number of business programs—Biz-in-a-Box and Micro Biz Navigator among them—as well as authoring the successful book How to Run a Business from the Kitchen Table. Barbara's story pays tribute to her mother's role in her education. It is little wonder that Barbara continues to value creativity and innovation in communication and education.*

When most adults I know talk about school days they recall lifelong school friends, sleep-overs, parties or that memorable teacher. Well, that all seems a bit foreign to me. I grew up in the New England district of New South Wales. My father managed sheep properties in the bush. The only other youngster I related to in the first fourteen years of my life was my brother who I never really got along with. As to my teacher—it was my mum.

I did have a teacher in the correspondence school where my lessons were mailed, but I don't remember a name. The only time I heard the voice of a teacher from the correspondence school was when I passed my Leaving Certificate at the age of sixteen.

I was going to a real school by then, in Wauchope, but I wanted to do Art and there was no teacher, so I was allowed to do it by correspondence. I was the first person to gain an A in this subject through the correspondence school and my teacher rang to congratulate me. WOW was that something!

What did I learn by doing my schooling this way, with mum for a teacher? Well I never learnt to be a bully or to be a bigot. We also did Sunday School by correspondence and I can honestly say when, finally, I did go to school, I did not understand why some people didn't like black people or those of a different religion. It was a foreign thought process for me. I was taught to like people for who they were and what they did, not to judge them according to colour, race or religion.

Home schooling had some wonderful advantages for me. I learnt to be self motivated and to be responsible; to manage my time efficiently; to think logically; to communicate effectively (all questions and answers from the correspondence teacher had to be written); to thirst for knowledge and books; to be persistent; to have patience; and above all, to think outside the square. I also learnt to love the power of words and drawings to describe my surroundings and to enjoy the wonderful land a fertile imagination can lead you into.

My parents never told me I couldn't do something so I grew up believing that if I wanted something badly enough, then I simply had to set my mind to it and work to get it. I also realised that working from home was no impediment to achieving the highest accolades. My passions have led me to become an author, an artist, a radio announcer. I run a home-based business and help others as a teacher and trainer. I have achieved all these things. The more I achieve the more I want to achieve. I can thank my mum, my teacher, for that.

Arlene Quinn

In 2000, after extensive experience in nursing and human resource leadership, **Arlene Quinn** established her speaking and consultancy business, People Performance Plus. Arlene works with a range of clients including people from the real estate and aged care sectors. Her story deals with a personal childhood experience and a sensitive teacher who helped to shape her attitude to life.

Miss Kaye spent time every day in her office with the door open. I wondered why. Had she not had enough of us kids when she spent all the school day in one room with four different primaries? I learnt many years later, as an adult, that she adored children and enjoyed the sound of our laughter so much she kept her door open deliberately to be there for us if we fell over or started squabbling.

She taught me that when you value someone or something you can feel hollow inside until that need has been fulfilled by reciprocation. How did this revelation come about? I had a close friend at school called Dorothy. One day Dorothy didn't come to school because, my mum said, she had scarlet fever. None of us knew what that really meant and how close she came to dying.

Miss Kaye asked us to consider what would be an appropriate gift for Dorothy to cheer her up; however, there was one proviso. Whatever we gave Dorothy could never be returned to us to play with again. Because of the infection, everything she touched had to be fumigated and her family were isolated in their home.

I really valued a little red-covered book that I knew Dorothy also liked. Miss Kaye talked to me about what it might mean if I never saw the book again and would I feel hollow inside without it. I decided that valuing Dorothy was much more important to me than any red-covered book. And you know, I didn't feel hollow once, or since.

— ❧ —

Teachers show empathy

Aldwyn Altuney

Aldwyn Altuney *is a photojournalist who has worked in the media in many parts of Australia for the past fifteen years. She edited the University of Canberra newspaper, Curio, and worked as a journalist at The Daily Mercury in Mackay, Coffs Harbour Advocate, Queensland Times in Ipswich among others. Aldwyn is a freelance writer for magazines and she has worked as a radio host and an actress. Based on the Gold Coast since 2000, Aldwyn is a corporate communications consultant and director of her company, AA Xpose Media, which offers public relations and photographic services.*

Everything happens for a reason. Whether we like it or not, every situation we encounter, every person we meet, everything we experience occurs for a reason. While we may not realise it at the time, the reason often becomes apparent down the track.

However, it's not what happens to us that matters, it's how we react to it. Attitude is everything. It's the difference between waking up smiling or frowning, going places or not going places, feeling fulfilled or empty.

The fact we are all here is a miracle. We are all gifts of life, the universe and all that is in it and we are all connected. The sooner we realise this and find our inner peace, the sooner we will work towards world peace.

We are all teachers and students at the same time. The more we learn, the more we realise there is to learn.

These are just some of my beliefs, which have been shaped in part by all the wonderful people I have encountered in my life. Being a photojournalist for fifteen years, working in the media in Sydney, Canberra, Brisbane, Mackay, Ipswich, Coffs Harbour, Toowoomba and the Gold Coast has been a real eye-opener.

I have had the good fortune to interview famous people like Russell Crowe, Hugh Jackman, Cyndi Lauper, Deborah Harry (Blondie), Jon Stevens (INXS), former Miss World Belinda Green, Richard Street (The Temptations), Jenny Morris, Jimmy Barnes, Wendy Matthews, Diesel, John 'Catfish' Purser (Johnny O'Keefe drummer), Suzi Quatro, Tim Freedman (The Whitlams), Marcia and Deni Hines, Sarina Russo, Claudia Karvan, Paul McDermott, Mikey Robins, The Sandman and Julie Anthony.

One thing I found with all these people is that they were passionate about what they did. They loved what they did. They were not wasting time in JOBS (Just Over Broke Situations) they did not enjoy. They followed their passions and it paid off. As they say, if you really enjoy what you are doing, you become good at it pretty quickly and the money comes.

I have also interviewed other influential people who have taught me a great deal. Kingscliff networking guru Robyn Henderson taught me the importance of making 'heart to heart connections'. Bali bomb blast victim Andrew Csabi taught me the strength of the human spirit to battle on for life despite the odds. National College of Business founders, Jon and Danyelle Mailer, taught me the importance of having a good attitude. Australian Institute of Fitness director Rowena Szeszeran-McEvoy taught me to give more than you receive to always receive more than you give. Gold Coast motivational speaker Keith Abraham taught me how to live my passions and Brisbane entrepreneur Sarina Russo taught me that nothing comes easy. Murwillumbah author Christine Murphy taught me it is not enough just knowing something, it is doing that brings results.

I have learned so much from so many people, I would need a whole book to list all of my teachers and life lessons.

To understand where I'm coming from, you need to know where I've been.

Born in Sydney's northern beaches in 1974, I had a different upbringing to most 'Aussie kids'. As a first generation Australian from wonderful mixed European heritage, I copped regular bouts of racism. My name was different (my Welsh first name comes from a close friend of my parents who died when mum was eight months pregnant with me). The delicious Mediterranean food I ate was different; I looked different, with naturally curly hair and my parents looked different to most Aussie kids' parents.

I started playing table tennis when I could barely see over the table, encouraged by my father, Michael, who was the high school champion in the southern seaside village of Iskenderun in Turkey where he grew up. I learned early on that persistence was required to win a game, as well as determination, hard work and the will to win. Confidence was also essential and that usually came with practice.

I found playing table tennis a great outlet to release the anger and frustrations I felt with the world and I developed a killer forehand smash. Along with my brother Nicholas, I soon began representing New South Wales in tournaments around Australia, and by the age of fourteen I was the Under 17 Australian champion. I also represented Mosman and Forest High Schools in netball, softball, tennis and athletics.

I was ranked in the top ten Australian table tennis players consistently from 1986 to 1995, winning the 1990 Australasian Youth singles and doubles titles.

I represented Australia in Finland, Sweden, Switzerland, Italy, England, China, Hong Kong, Korea, New Caledonia and Japan.

I beat the number thirty two in the world as a sixteen year-old in the Italian Open Championships in 1990 when the top senior Australian female player was ranked 230 in the world.

These are all great achievements I feel very proud of but more than anything, being ambitious in sport has made me ambitious in all other areas of my life.

It has helped me cope with very stressful work situations and taught me not to take people's anger personally.

One of my most significant teachers has been my father, who grew up rejected in the country he was born in because he had a Ukranian father.

Since the Turks and Ukraines/ Russians were at war for 400 years, the latter were always seen as traitors in Turkey. My father felt strong discrimination all his life in Turkey, even though he never knew his dad.

My father often said, 'There are hidden rules in society. People are judged by the way they look, dress and behave and it's important to notice the way people act in certain situations. Sometimes you have to accept that people have to experience things for themselves.'

'Parents have the right to say when they disagree with something their child is doing but they must realise their children need to make decisions for themselves.' As our life expectancy is too short to experience everything first hand, he said it was wise to learn from other people's experiences.

Former tennis professional, Dream Maker Enterprises founder, Scott Groves, who once said, `If you don't know where you're going, any road will get you nowhere,' gave an excellent image of this recently. In his book, *The Power of Subconscious Goal Setting*, he wrote, 'There will be some struggles that we simply must fight on our own. It is these struggles that give us the strength to know that we can survive anything.' He said a butterfly had to fight its way through a tiny opening in the cocoon to fly and if we tried to help it escape, we would cripple it.

Former world ironman champion, Trevor Hendy, who is based on the Gold Coast, said the more he moved ahead in life, the more people would try to push him back. This caused him to become harder on the outside, be more distrustful of people and work even harder to push ahead.

What he has realised now that he has retired from competing is that what's happening on the inside gets buried by the rest of life. 'We ignore what really matters', he said.

'I love people, I love caring. I started to compete to care more but my relationship at the time suffered. My love was huge, the fights were huge and the misunderstandings were massive.'

It was only when someone said, 'Whatever is going on in your heart with your ex will carry through in your current relationship', that he realised what was happening.

Trevor said 'The common denominator is yourself. I started to look at how much I was blaming my partner. By fully experiencing what I felt, I realised it never came out.'

His speech moved to tears most of the audience at the March 2005 Women In Tourism meeting at Currumbin Sanctuary. Trevor touched a part of us we often don't see. We are all born with a lot of love in our hearts and as we grow, we often become harder by nature—less trusting, less loving, less caring. We feel people hurt us, so we build walls around our hearts. But then we realise, no-one can hurt us unless we let them. Whenever we feel down, we must ask ourselves, 'What is the lesson to be learned here?'

And if we look down deep enough, we will often find that the answer lies within us.

Author Contact Details

Kerrie Akkermans
1/813 South Road
Clarence Gardens SA 5039
Tel 08 8338 5522
Fax 08 8371 2434
Mob 0417 872 389
akkerman@senet.com.au
www.akkermans.speakerdirect.com.au

Aldwyn Altuney
AA Xposé Media
PO Box 114
Southport BC Qld 4215
Mob 0409 895 055
aaxpose@yahoo.com.au

Peter Burke
pxburke@bigpond.net.au

Gerard Byrne
PO Box 3459
Hermit Park Qld 4812
Tel 07 4722 2517
Mob 0417 770 340
suncity@beyond.net.au

Bronwen Campbell
bc@bronwencampbell.com
www.bronwencampbell.com

Judith Campbell
Suite 2, 63 Rosstown Road
Carnegie Vic 3163

Rachel Cliff
info@heartharmony.com.au

Teagan Cliff
info@heartharmony.com.au

Rhonda Coles
Mob 0421 823 480
rfcoles@optusnet.com.au

Shirley Dalton
PO Box 529
Charlestown NSW 2290
Tel 02 4920 9808
sirdalt@bigpond.com

Maggie Dent
www.esteemplus.com
www.calmingkids.com

Lisa Dunn
tldunn@bigpond.com

Jo Eady
Rural Women in Business Global Learning Centre
PO Box 6133
Fairfield Gardens Qld 4103
Tel 07 3848 2890
jo@rwib.com
www.rwib.com

Jenni Erbel
GPO Box 1164
Brisbane Qld 4001
jenni@wealthbydesign.com.au
www.wealthbydesign.com.au

Leanne Farmiloe
Mob 0407 785 227
bowbird@linkt.com.au

Joyce Fewtrell
3/38-40 Bridge Street
Epping NSW 2121

Jack Fraenkel
Mob 0419 444 240
jackfraenkel@motivatories.com.au
www.motivatories.com.au

Barbara Gabogrecan
Mob 0418 106 133
barbara@micronavigator.com.au
www.micronavigator.com.au

Chadia Gedeon
Mob 0438 084 413
chadia@bigpond.com

Joan Griffiths
252 North Star Resort
Hastings Point NSW 2489

Rachel Hawken
2/222 Marine Parade
Kingscliff NSW 2487

Nina Hope
nina@wealthbydesign.com.au
www.wealthbydesign.com.au

Jodie Hudson
Jodie@riseinternational.com.au
www.riseinternational.com.au

Celeste Kirby-Brown
celestekb@talentmanagement.com.au

Nana Yaa Larbi
Tel 0044 20 756 0991
nanayaa@larbi.com

Jason Lea
Mob 0414 362 364
jdlea@dlea.com.au

Lizzy Malcolm
lizmalcolm2003@yahoo.com.au

Judy Mason
Tel 07 5590 4152

Cat Matson
cat@catmatson.com.au

Rod Matthews
rmatthews@impacthpt.com.au

Cheryl Norkus
PO Box 145
Sale Vic 3850

Ricky Nowak
ricky@confidentcomms.com.au
www.confidentcomms.com.au

Arlene Quinn
Mob 0402 272 868
coach@arlenequinn.com

Tory Richards
trichards@pearlproperty.com.au

Kylie Saunder
Naturally on Chapel
Level 1/553 Chapel Street
South Yarra Vic 3141
Tel 03 9827 6426

Gary Summers
Tel 02 4389 1262
Mob 0411 340 439
garsum@ozemail.com.au

Pam Tate
Tel 02 9743 0061
pamtate@optusnet.com.au

Megan Tough
megan@megantough.com
www.megantough.com

Merilyn Wallace
Correct Editing
correctediting@telstra.com

Duff Watkins
Tel +61 2 9411 4472
dw@execsearch.com.au
www.execsearch.com.au

Cherie Woolven
Tel 08 8821 2539
cheriesinsights@netyp.com.au

About Robyn Henderson and Sea Change Publishing

As a Global Networking Specialist, Robyn Henderson has built a successful career across ten countries speaking and writing about her passion—networking. Robyn has successfully self-published six of her seven books on business networking, self-promotion and self-esteem building.

Travelling the world, Robyn met many interesting people and she encouraged them to share their stories either through books, articles, e-books or on film. She realised that the thought of writing a book often overwhelmed many of these fascinating people—yet, she knew their stories had to be told.

Being a master solution provider, Robyn offered workshops in Australia and New Zealand on writing non-fiction books and in 2004 she established Sea Change Publishing. Using her networking skills Robyn has brought together a stable of experts to assist with every facet of book production: ghostwriters, editors, typesetters, graphic designers, literary stylists, proofreaders, printers, marketing experts, public relations consultants and event managers.

Robyn has formed a dream team of innovative thinkers who are available to brainstorm ideas on book concepts, content viability, target audiences and potential global markets for budding authors unsure of the writing and publishing process. Sea Change Publishing can project manage your book from concept to completion.

For information about Sea Change Publishing, please visit
www.seachangepublishing.com.au
or email
robyn@seachangepublishing.com.au

To book Robyn for a keynote presentation, training seminar,
half or full day workshop, nationally or internationally, please
contact

Robyn Henderson
Networking to Win
PO Box 1596
Kingscliff NSW 2487
Tel: 61 2 6674 0211
Fax: 61 2 6674 0233

robyn@networkingtowin.com.au
www.networkingtowin com au
www.robynhenderson.com

Order Form

Copies of this book and its companion volume are available from Sea Change Publishing.

Fax order to 02 6674 0233

☐ Please rush me the following: (includes GST)

☐ 1 book $27.50 plus $5.00 P&H Total $32.50

☐ 5 books $99.00 plus $10.00 P&H Total $109.00

☐ 10 books $165.00 plus $15.00 P&H Total $180.00

☐ 25 books $385.00 plus $25.00 P&H Total $410.00

☐ 100 books $990.00 plus $50.00 P&H Total $1040.00

☐ Volume order - price on application - please provide price for .... books

ORDER FORM YES I want to order
WHAT MY FAVOURITE TEACHER TAUGHT ME ☐ Volume 1 ☐ Volume 2

Name: .... Today's date: ....

School/Organisation: ....

Phones/s: ....

Postal Address: ....

Suburb: .... State: .... Postcode: ....

Email: .... Country: (if not Australia) ....

METHOD OF PAYMENT:

I agree to send payment within 7 days of invoice receipt.

☐ Visa ☐ Mastercard ☐ Bankcard ☐ Cheque ☐ Please invoice me.

Card Number: .... Expiry: ..../...........

Name on Card: .... Signature:...

Fax or mail to:

Networking to Win ABN 11 842 064 583
PO Box 1596, Kingscliff NSW 2487
Phone: 02 6674 0211 • **Fax:** 02 6674 0233
Email: robyn@networkingtowin.com.au
Web: www.networkingtowin.com.au

Sea Change Publishing

OFFICE USE ONLY
☐ post product

Fax: 02 6674 0233 • www.networkingtowin.com.au • www.seachangepublishing.com.au

✷ **Volume Two** ✷